Natalie Boehm

Author, Disability Advocate and
Strategic Planner

The Formula for Success

Taking Your Life and Career to the Next Level

Legal Disclaimer

THE FORMULA FOR SUCCESS Copyright © 2023 Natalie Boehm. All rights reserved worldwide.

No part of this material may be used, reproduced, distributed or transmitted in any form and by any means whatsoever, including without limitation photocopying, recording or other electronic or mechanical methods or by any information storage and retrieval system, without the prior written permission from the author, except for brief excerpts in a review. This book is intended to provide general information only. Neither the author nor publisher provides any legal or other professional advice. If you need professional advice, you should seek advice from the appropriate licensed professional. This book does not provide complete information on the subject matter covered. This book is not intended to address specific requirements, either for an individual or an organization. This book is intended to be used only as a general guide, and not as a sole source of information on the subject matter. While the author has undertaken diligent efforts to ensure accuracy, there is no guarantee of accuracy or of no errors, omissions or typographical errors. Any slights of people or organizations are unintentional. The author and publisher shall have no liability or responsibility to any person or entity and hereby disclaim all liability, including without limitation, liability for consequential damages regarding any claim, loss or damage that may be incurred, or alleged to have been incurred, directly or indirectly, arising out of the information provided in this book.

Published by Magnetic Entrepreneur Inc.™
https://www.facebook.com/magneticentrepreneur
www.linkedin.com/in/magneticentrepreneur
E-Mail: magneticpublishing2017@gmail.com
Website: magnetic-entrepreneur.com

Copyright © 2023 by NATALIE BOEHM
All rights reserved. No part of this publication may be reproduced or transmitted in any form or by any means, electronic, or mechanical, including photocopying, recording, or by any information storage and retrieval system.

Dedication

I dedicate this book to my husband Tobias and sons Edward and Anthony for all of their love and support. Thank you for seeing past my imperfections and seeing what I truly can contribute to help others.

I dedicate this book also to the epilepsy community with the goal of showing those battling epilepsy that epilepsy does not have to control your every move in life. If I had listened to the toxicity of others, I would not have had the honor of writing this book. Learn your strengths, show others what you are truly capable of, and most importantly, love yourself.

Acknowledgements

I would like to thank my mentor Robert J. Moore for all of his support. Robert has never judged me for having epilepsy and has seen the potential I have to be a productive member of society. Without the support of Robert, this project would not have been possible. Thank you, Robert, for all of your knowledge and support. I look forward to continuing to work together and the difference we can make for others.

I would like to thank Magnetic Entrepreneur Inc.™ for publishing my book and allowing a dream of mine to come true. Thank you for all of your support in helping to make this project possible.

I would like to thank Dr. Ian Bone for writing the foreword for this book and for your friendship. I greatly admire and appreciate everything you have done for the epilepsy community and your dedication to helping remove the stigma that has had a hold on our community for so long.

I would like to thank my neurologist Dr. George Nune for all his support in helping me to achieve wellness at a very challenging time in my life. Thank you for advocating for me and supporting me in reaching my goals. I promise to continue to stay focused, face my challenges in a positive way, and set an example for others.

Finally, I would like to thank the readers of this book. Please see this as more than a book, but as a resource for you to come back to again and again. Knowledge is power, and the most important person you can invest in is you.

~ v ~

Thank you again to everyone for your support. You each played an important role in making this possible.

Sincerely,

Natalie L. Boehm

TABLE OF CONTENTS

Contents

FOREWORD

More and more, people are taking their wellness and happiness into their own hands, and there are many books available that aim to help them take their lives and careers to the next level. What is it about this author's book that sets it apart from many others? Natalie Boehm has evidently "walked the walk" by virtue of navigating the hazardous route with significant health issues to become the President and Founder of the not-for-profit organisation the *Defeating Epilepsy Foundation*. She defines herself as follows: "I am an advocate for individuals and families who are battling epilepsy. I was diagnosed with epilepsy at the age of two due to a traumatic brain injury. For many years epilepsy had control of me, limiting me in what I could do with my life. After years of battling seizures and going through many combinations of treatments, I made up my mind that epilepsy was not going to control me. I would not allow the stigma that is associated with epilepsy to take over my life." It is this resolve that legitimises her right to provide advice as well as underpin her books, aims and objectives. Throughout, Natalie uses a narrative of personal experiences to introduce the reader to guidance, accessible resources, understandable science and lists of "things to remember." The book starts with Natalie's own intimate history and ends having armed the reader with her wisdom and resources on how to continue the journey thereafter.

In setting the scene, the book commences by emphasizing the importance of breaking away from the toxicity that ill health, with its inherent negative experiences, can create. Her truism that "if you consume toxicity, you become toxic" is central to this powerful introductory chapter. Nothing is spared here in her personal account of growing up with epilepsy. The negative impact of the condition upon schooling, family relationships, unsatisfactory health professional contacts, drug side effects and seizure-related injuries will be all too familiar to those who live with epilepsy, as will the toxicity, bitterness and depression that so often result. Natalie discusses the challenging impact of personally facing the benefits system, the important support Tobias, her life partner, has proved to be, as well as the experiences of them dealing with illness and hemophilia within their own sons. She also outlines the complex and frustrating problems of access and costs within her own healthcare system. Despite all these troublesome experiences, she states that it is critical to well-being to champion over negativity, face the journey and remember that you "deserve to be happy, healthy and successful." Whether healthy or not, the author stresses how education is central to success and describes how her own foundation provides college scholarships. What follows thereafter is a well-resourced guide to USA Education law, giving advice on the advantages of internships and mentoring, with a breakdown of the financial costs that might be incurred. While stressing the importance of education, she counsels that careful research is advised, before setting out on the journey, to avoid unrealistic goals and setting oneself up for confidence-sapping failure.

Personal and professional goal setting is prefaced by "the secret of getting ahead is getting started" from the ever-quotable Mark Twain. The author comments that when setting up and pursuing goals, things do not necessarily always go to plan. Here she draws upon personal experience to underpin the advice on needing to stay flexible. The physical tools of goal setting, along with the importance of SMART, are explained as is the value of acquiring social skills, the role of conformity, emotional intelligence and the concept of respectability. The latter is illustrated with an account of a seizure occurring during her studentship, which led to negativity from others who had witnessed it. This chapter concludes with advice on conflict resolution strategies within the workplace.

To facilitate the growth of a career and improve upon goal-achieving, resources are needed. Understanding how to network and the role of social media in doing so is critical to success, as is becoming aware of what type of learner you are. This chapter is well-resourced and provides key online links. Readers will be able to easily identify their type of learning and access resources accordingly. Here the roles of career coach, mentor and sponsor are discussed in detail, along with the relative merits of each.

Chapter five introduces the reader to the many methods of communication and their relative importance. Each, whether interpersonal, small group or public, requires verbal and non-verbal skills. Sustained business success cannot happen without being a good communicator and using all forms of mass media knowledgeably. A useful guide to the pros and cons of various social media platforms follows. The author's comments, the signposting to resources to improve communication skills and her advice in avoiding workplace gossip are invaluable. The destructive effect of the latter is emphasised.

Next follows an account of how to focus on overcoming past negative experiences that might hold the individual back from achieving planned goals. Once more, personal experiences of low self-esteem and managing post-traumatic stress disorder (PTSD) are used to illustrate how challenges can be faced positively.

Invaluable is the introduction of the role of positive psychology (a concept that will be new to many) in character strengthening, how to achieve the fine balance between being selfish and selfless and a highly informative account of imposter syndrome and dimensions of wellness. The author's clear text is supplemented with a guide to any relevant online resources.

The commonality of fear of failure is stressed along with the long-term health consequences that can result. The anatomy and physiology of fear and stress are described in lay terms, and the benefits of positive thinking to overcome fear and stress are helpfully discussed. Atychiphobia, the abnormal, unwarranted and persistent fear of failure, and atelophobia, the fear of not being good enough or imperfection, are differentiated and how the latter may result in micromanagement and how this can best be avoided. The take-home message is how not to be overtaken by fear and not allow it to reduce life opportunities. Fear can inhibit taking a risk. If you don't take the shot, you will never know how far the ball might have gone. The message is to be prepared for the occasional failure, handle it, learn from it and move on but don't let it inhibit enterprise.

The value of sharing a story follows. Here the reader is informed on the importance of authenticity and that sharing experiences with others gives the storyteller a voice, re-affirms values, and often provides a therapeutic closure. The author recounts her own story about applying for a job and the negative impact that disclosing her epilepsy had. Sharing this with others, who may have been in a similar situation, can be beneficial to all. She tells about searching for and finding a new neurologist and how this positively banished certain preconceived notions of health professionals. Being authentic is essential to storytelling, as is the passion and honesty that shines through the story. The benefits of writing down, or telling stories in relation to the experiences of living with a long-term health condition, are increasingly recognised as both therapeutic and instructive.

The concluding chapters pull together what has gone before, preparing the reader for success and suggesting how to consolidate achievements and plan to reach the next level. Natalie writes, "Now that we have talked about the tools and resources needed to reach goals, what do we do to use them effectively?" She adds that this involves stepping out of the comfort zone by addressing personal micro habits such as learning to say "no," being less reactive, sharing ideas and being approachable. Developing a social support system, the role of philanthropy and the concept of corporate social responsibility are each discussed. To be creative, the reader is advised to acknowledge when change is needed and to step out of her comfort zone in order to achieve this and also, sagely, that as your business grows, "Do not forget to take care of yourself." The concluding chapter introduces the reader to branding, cautioning that "If you don't brand yourself, others in time will." The critical advice on overcoming the fear of failure is reinforced, and the reader is encouraged to develop strategic thinking skills, focus on customers and clients, and consider the value of high stretch (high risk) goals. Finally, the issue of legacy is answered by the author herself, stating that "My goal in creating my organization is that I want the next generation dealing with epilepsy not to face the same hardship and discrimination that I have."

This is a remarkable book on so many different levels. The author tells her honest and often harrowing personal story alongside wise advice and valuable referenced resources. Her

"Things to remember" at the conclusion of each chapter cement contents in the reader's memory. That her journey through life has experienced discrimination and stigmatization is evident from the stories told. Despite the challenges that Natalie Boehm has faced, she has created an organization, the *Defeating Epilepsy Foundation*, whose purpose is to support those with epilepsy that have shared similar journeys. In this voyage, she has been blessed with the support of Tobias, her life partner. Sadly, for many with epilepsy, finding such support does not come easily and can prove problematic. The style of the book is easy on the reader's eye with, at the end of each chapter, a list of things to remember and many referenced online resources. She states that "By finishing this book, you should have taken the first steps in helping yourself grow and do well for yourself and others." This book is certainly a valuable resource to help all, and not necessarily just those who live with a long-term health condition, set and achieve their goals.

Dr. Ian Bone

Helensburgh UK

Dr. Ian Bone is a retired neurologist with over 40 years of personal and professional experience helping people with epilepsy. He is the author of *Sacred Lives: an account of the history, cultural associations, and social impact of epilepsy.*

Introduction

The Formula for Success provides information and resources to help you take your life and career to the next level. With information based on education, goal setting, strategic planning, career resources, communication, and well-being, *The Formula for Success* will help guide you and help you to set realistic goals and take different approaches to achieve what you want out of life.

The Formula for Success focuses on important issues such as removing toxicity from your life, the importance of education, personal vs. professional goals, climate vs. culture in the workforce, facing challenges, overcoming the fear of failure, embracing vulnerability, how to network, the importance of sharing your story, and the importance of branding yourself. *The Formula for Success* is a book that any professional can use to create positive changes in their career and find ways to let go of negativity and take a more positive approach to their personal and professional lives.

Whether you are a college student or a CEO of a company, *The Formula for Success* can guide you as you create goals to better yourself, move to a higher level, and find balance in what you do.

BIO

Natalie Boehm is an author, disability advocate, and strategic planner. She is the president and founder of *The Defeating Epilepsy Foundation,* providing advocacy and educational services for individuals and families who are battling epilepsy. Natalie was diagnosed with epilepsy at the age of two and has not allowed epilepsy to define who she is as a person and professional. Natalie obtained her master's degree in business administration from the University of Redlands and has multiple certificates in nonprofit and organizational leadership, as well as social entrepreneurship.

Chapter 1

How to Break Away from Toxicity

"Life is short. Don't waste it with negative people who don't appreciate you. Keep them in your heart but keep them out of your life."- Anonymous

"If you attach to the negative behavior of others, it brings you down to their level."- Guru Singh

"The less you respond to negative people, the more powerful your life will become."- Robert E. Baine, Jr.

Toxicity is defined as an extremely harsh, malicious, or harmful quality (Merriam-Webster, 2022). We all come into contact with toxic people or situations in our lifetime. What is important is how we face it or deal with it. I have faced a lot of toxicity in my lifetime. Reviewing the quotes above, they all speak a truth; if you consume toxicity, you become toxic. For you to get ahead, toxicity cannot be a part of your life. As I share my journey with you in this chapter, I want you to think of any challenges you have had or any toxicity in your life. At the end of this book, I want you to have the strength to remove toxicity from your life, gain the strength and confidence to work towards what you want and achieve the dreams you have.

My journey began as a young child battling a neurological disorder. I was diagnosed with epilepsy at the age of two due to a traumatic brain injury. I was too young to remember the event; however, that one event made a major impact on my life, creating a very difficult path to follow. Epilepsy is a neurological disorder that results in an individual having seizures. There are many different types of epilepsy and seizures, making it a complex condition. Epilepsy affected my family in a negative way. My mother was a single mother due to having an affair with my father, who was married. Once becoming pregnant with me, he distanced himself away from my mother. After my diagnosis, he decided he was going to focus on his marriage, and his family made it clear they did not want my mother and me to be a part of their lives.

My early childhood was a big blur due to the medication that I was put on by my neurologist. I was prescribed phenobarbital, a strong barbiturate that was used to control seizures. I was prescribed ninety milligrams a day, making simple tasks such as playing, doing schoolwork, and socializing a challenge. Due to the extreme exhaustion I felt on the medication, I became frustrated and overwhelmed easily, resulting in me crying a lot of the time. I was labeled as a difficult child rather than one who was heavily medicated. Despite my challenges, I did well in school and was never placed in any special education program. I was given the same opportunities as the other children in the classroom.

Dealing with a chronic illness is challenging for anyone, but for someone who must be a caregiver, it is even more challenging. My mother relied on her family to help, which they did. My grandmother did not help my mother in advocating for me but took control as if I were her daughter and not granddaughter. It caused a lot of resentment and was the beginning of my mother and I not establishing a healthy relationship. My mother wanted to get away from her family and met my stepfather, who is an insurance agent and property manager. Clearly, from the beginning, there were signs that he was an abusive person. Even before my mother married my stepfather, I feared him, not knowing how he would react. My mother started dating my stepfather when I was eight after accepting a position at a computer company he owned at the time. The relationship moved fast, and a year later, my mother and I moved in with him into a home across the street from his parents' house. My mother's parents found out that he was physically abusing me to the point where he was leaving marks on me. Furious, they confronted him, telling him to stay away from me. It did nothing but make him feel more powerful, as he instructed my mother to cut off ties with her parents and not allow me to see them. I was told that I would never see my grandparents again. It was traumatizing; my grandparents were my parents to me due to being abandoned by my father and not bonding with my mother. My seizures increased, and my health deteriorated. My aunt finally convinced my mother to come to a middle ground for the sake of my well-being. My mother agreed, and my grandparents were allowed to see me again. My stepfather played mind games, making it clear that if my grandparents did not do things his way, he would pull me out of their lives again. It was a toxic situation in which my stepfather abused many of my loved ones, and my mother supported him, feeling if she kept him happy, things would fall into place in time.

Things did not fall into place, though; in fact, they became worse the older I became. My mother became pregnant with my sister, and my mother married my stepfather in July 1988. In March of 1989, my mother gave birth to my sister. The first time I saw my sister at two days old was one of the happiest moments in my life. My mother made an appointment for me to be able to come up to the hospital to meet her. I remember the nurse helping me hold my sister and so many happy emotions going through me. I was now a big sister, something I never thought I would be. I looked up and saw how angry my stepfather was as I bonded with her. My mother kept telling him to relax, but I could clearly see he did not want me there. It was not until I was an adult that I realized what caused his anger that day.

A year later, in October 1990, my brother was born. My mother was clearly exhausted with two new babies, a chronically ill child, and an abusive husband who did not help her in any way. While my mother was pregnant, my stepfather was having affairs, one particular with an employee of his who my mother had hired. It caused my mother to have severe post-partum depression and be admitted for a psych evaluation. I cannot remember how many days my mother was there, but I missed her terribly and did not understand why she was there. It was around this time I noticed that my stepfather was abusing all of us, just at different levels. I just didn't realize at that point how severe it was going to get or how long it was going to last.

The same year that my brother was born was the same year I would truly be tested when it came to having epilepsy. Phenobarbital was no longer working, and the neurologist put me on Depakote to control my seizures. Depakote has a long history of negative side effects and causes birth defects. Within a short time, I gained twenty pounds, and my hair started to fall out. Instead of talking to the doctor about the negative side effects, my stepfather started using the side effects against me. He would call me negative names such as "fat fuck" on a regular basis. My mother's response to it was, "just lose the weight, and he will stop." It didn't stop, and things went downhill. I would steal food he did not want me to have to feel in control, causing me to gain more weight. I would become frightened after eating a lot and vomit, hoping it would not affect me. My grades started to go down, and my teachers could clearly see something was not right. I made the mistake of telling one of my teachers about my situation at home. Instead of reporting the abuse, they called my parents and let them know what I said. I received a severe beating for it and was told to go back to school and tell the teachers that I lied to them. After that, I knew I had no one I could confide in, that I was alone.

The next four years on Depakote were the hardest years of my life. I started throwing my medication out and forcing myself to have seizures, hoping I would go into status epilepticus and not survive. I wanted more than anything to die; the only thing that kept me from truly wanting to go through with suicide was I did not want to hurt my sister and brother. I felt as long as my parents were targeting me and not them, they would at least be safe. Along with not being able to trust my parents, I started to sense something was not right between the neurologist and me. When I was having migraines which triggered my seizures, he told my mother to give me

Tylenol and Sudafed to sleep it off. It put me into statis and almost killed me a few times. Years later, after he retired and I moved to another neurologist, he let me know that my former neurologist was experimenting to see what the effects of Sudafed had on people with epilepsy. He received a grant for this research project. Never did he tell my parents that this was part of a research project; my parents thought they were complying with my treatment. When I found out about this, I felt that my former neurologist did not see me as a human being but as a guinea pig to experiment on for profit gain.

I felt that Depakote was going to kill me. Two weeks before my sixteenth birthday, I met with my neurologist. I told him I would no longer comply with my treatment. I told him that if he didn't take me off the medication, I would not make it to my sixteenth birthday and that I was not joking. He took me seriously and put me on Felbatol. Felbatol attacked my white blood cells and cut my level in half. Something as small as a sinus infection would put me into status epilepticus, and I would be in the hospital for days. I had to come off Felbatol and go on Dilantin and then Tegretol. Every time I changed my medication, my personality changed due to the side effects. Anticonvulsant medication suppresses the central nervous system, which causes depression. Living in an abusive environment, I became angry and aggressive over time. I was at the point where I no longer felt safe in the house, yet I did not know how I would get my medication if I left. The final straw for me was my stepfather attacked me one night. He grabbed me and ripped my shirt open. I was afraid he was going to sexually assault me. I shoved him off me and hit him in the face. The look on his face was priceless. He never thought

I would have the courage to fight back. My mother came to his defence, furious that I would stand up for myself.

I knew I had to get out of the house. I went to my grandparents, letting them know the severity of the abuse that was taking place. My grandparents allowed me to move in. For the next couple of years, I made a lot of bad choices. I did not focus on college; in fact, after a couple of semesters, I quit school and got a full-time job at a grocery store. I felt I had to do this in order to get my medication. In a short time, however, I knew I didn't want to spend the rest of my life in grocery retail. It was at that point I knew in order to heal, I had to go back to school. I started going to school at night to study to become a paralegal. My dream, when I was younger was to become a trial attorney. My stepfather and mother did everything they could to drill into my head that people of my kind did not become attorneys and that no one would hire someone of my kind. I made up my mind that I was going to be educated and independent. I was determined to survive and be able to care for myself.

The next two years were very challenging as I worked full-time and went to school full-time. I was having complex partial seizures rather than tonic-clonic. Thanks to Tegretol, I have not had a tonic-clonic seizure since 1995. Tegretol has been a lifesaver for me and has allowed me to live as normal of a life as possible. I was hiding from my neurologist that my seizures were taking place. During the last year of school, I almost died from a miscarriage. I had been in a relationship with my boyfriend for three years, and it was very painful for us. In time, it ended our relationship because he saw how hurt I was and did not know what to do to help me. I confided in my mother about the loss and that I was depressed. Her response was, "Well, it's never happened to me, so what do you want me to do?". The same level of coldness that I received as a child from my mother continued. At this point in my life, I wanted a relationship with my mother, and I wanted us to heal. I didn't see at the time that my mother did not want the same. I took on a position as a paralegal working in commercial real estate, removing liens off of properties. I became part-time at the grocery store to keep my cobra. I was scared that in a year and a half, if I could not find a full-time job, it was going to be a death sentence for me not being able to get my medication. I was on Tegretol and Lamictal, and in time my neurologist added Topamax to the mix. I was seriously overmedicated and exhausted from working seven days a week and hiding that my seizures were taking place. It got to the point where I couldn't hide them anymore. One afternoon in my apartment, I went face-first into the floor and had a seizure. When it ended, I carefully got off the floor and didn't realize the injury I had sustained to my face. The next morning getting ready for work, I saw the right side of my face. It looked like someone had punched me. I did my best to hide it, but even after putting makeup on, it was visible. My co-workers thought I had been assaulted by my ex-boyfriend and told me to file a police report. I told them he did not assault me, yet I didn't want to tell them I had a seizure. I went to the neurologist and broke down, acknowledging what had been taking place. I also let him know I couldn't move forward, that I was really trying to survive, but I was exhausted, and I didn't know what to do. I was placed under a 5150 order at Buffalo General Hospital. I spent three days there, and the best way to explain that a psych ward is like going to jail, but you are not staying in a cell. I felt like I was going to lose it and did what I could to fake that I was better. I left the hospital, convincing them I was okay, yet I wanted more than anything to end my life still. I just decided it was worth the risk rather than being hospitalized.

My mother pressured me to apply for disability, and I gave in. It was the most degrading thing I had ever gone through. Having social workers talk down to me and scold me, specialists looking at me like I was faking what I was going through. I was still in college, refusing to quit despite being advised by my neurologist and attorney. I was determined to get better; I didn't want an SSI or SSDI check. My neurologist was at his wit's end with me for refusing to comply. During one visit, he looked at me and asked, "Why can't you be a good girl and just go on disability?" I didn't answer him, but that was the starting point at which I realized I had to take control of my life. I couldn't rely on others; I couldn't feel sorry for myself. I just had to work hard and survive, like everyone else in society. When my denial letter came, it was the happiest moment of my life. I threw it in the garbage and made it clear to my mother that I would risk dying than going in front of a judge and begging for support. She was furious that I refused to fight it or make an attempt to find a group home in which to live. I made it clear to her that I was not the property of the American taxpayer, and I would rather die young giving one hundred percent than being in a group home and wondering if I had just tried, could I have been successful.

After graduating with my bachelor's degree, I went back to my grandparents and found a temp job with the SBA under the Disaster Services program. It was a great opportunity for me to gain some experience and strengthen my resume. I had two goals at that time, to establish a career and to heal. A friend of mine suggested I start dating again. I had been single for over three years and was hesitant to start a new relationship. I finally gave in after many of my friends suggested that I should try. I placed an ad on Yahoo Personals, thinking nothing was going to come of it, but my friends couldn't say I didn't try. Within a few months, I saw a gentleman who was a research student at the University of Buffalo. There was something about him; I just didn't know what. I reached out to him to see if he would respond. A couple of days later, we started talking. We slowly became friends, and he invited me to meet him at a restaurant and to see a show at Shea's Theater with him. I drove down to the restaurant, nervous as can be, thinking, would he really show up? I arrived, and thirty minutes later, he did as well. The first time I looked into his eyes, I thought he looked so sweet. He was six foot one, huge compared to me at five foot four. Yet he came off so gentle despite his size. Little did I know during this date that in a couple of years, this date would lead to me marrying Tobias.

My husband Tobias has been more to me than a husband. He is my best friend, my soulmate, and due to my health, my caregiver. If Tobias had not become part of my life, I know for sure I would not be alive writing this book. While we were engaged, Tobias and I moved in together, and he encouraged me to get counseling to help with the trauma I had endured from my family and epilepsy. He would go at times with me to my sessions and realized how much the trauma had played a part in my personality and how I reacted to things. I had never had anyone be as supportive as Tobias had been then and even more now. I was worried our relationship would not last long-term due to my family acting rudely to him. Tobias is a very educated individual. He grew up in Germany in a village called Muhldörf, which is an hour to an hour and a half south of Munich in Bavaria. His parents were financially well off and, when younger, had multiple properties throughout the world, went on many trips, and lived a life many only wished they could have. The moment my mother found out about Tobias' parent's wealth, she was trying to do everything she could to cozy up to him. It was a turnoff because he could clearly see she was not judging him on how he would treat me, but what could she get out of him. I told Tobias about my family's past and assured him that I loved him for who he was, not how big his bank account was. He realized that I was nothing like my mother and that I was not with him due to his family. My in-laws picked up on my mother's behavior and were very concerned. I could sense they did not want the wedding to happen, yet did not try to stop us from marrying. Tobias and I were married on March 31, 2006. It was a moment in my life that I thought would never happen. I am beyond grateful for all the years I have had with Tobias because he has never judged me for having epilepsy and, in my darkest of times, has been my rock.

Once married, Tobias and I did everything to support one another. He applied for his green card, and we complied with everything we had to do. I was frustrated because many of the graduate programs I wanted to apply for were out of state, and I was not allowed to live separately from Tobias due to the green card requirements that we were under. When the 2008 economic crash happened, it really took a toll on us. Tobias was doing everything to get through graduate school. He was working on his Ph.D. in oral biology and a certificate in periodontics. Being in two programs at the same time was taking a toll on his health. He lost a lot of weight and was taking on too much. I did everything to support him and get him through his challenging time. He finished his Ph.D. and perio certificate and accepted a position at Western University of Health Sciences in Pomona, California. Moving from New York to California was an amazing experience. We took a week to drive across the county and see parts of America I thought I would never see.

We arrived in Southern California and moved into an apartment in Upland. Tobias was working crazy hours, but his health was improving. Mine, on the other hand, was deteriorating due to being homesick. I was missing New York and my friends greatly. I found myself sinking into a severe depression and knew I had to try to adjust to the new culture I was in. If you have ever lived on the east coast and west coast of America, you know firsthand that the cultures are the opposite of one another. On the east coast, we are very straightforward and blunt; what you see is what you get. The west coast people are very passive-aggressive; what they tell you and what they tell others are two different things. Being in Southern California was challenging due to that, and I can't tell you how many times I wanted to get on a plane and go home. I would not leave Tobias as he started his career. My friends did everything they could to help me adjust, but I wanted more than anything to be with them again.

Tobias and I focused on building a life together. We decided to start a family, and my neurologist helped me to prepare my body for pregnancy. I came off my Topamax and cut my Lamictal and Carbamazepine doses in half. For three months, I was taking a prenatal supplement along with 4000 mcg of folic acid. It did not take long after the neurologist and OB/GYN gave the okay to try that Tobias and I conceived. We were happy to be starting a family, something we had questioned would even be possible with my epilepsy. In the beginning, everything was going well. I was not having seizures, and our son was developing well. Two months before I was due to give birth, I had bleeding complications and ended up on bed rest. I didn't know at the time, but I have a bleeding condition called hemophilia A, which affects around twenty thousand Americans, and two hundred thousand people globally. I had no idea that this bleeding condition was going to have a major impact on my family.

Eddie was born on November 9, 2011. Tobias and I were overjoyed to have Eddie in our lives. Never did I feel I would have the opportunity to become a mother. Having Eddie come into my life made me want to become a better person. It was the first step in realizing that in order to be happy, I had to get rid of the toxicity in my life. It was easier said than done because, at that point, I still wanted to be in a relationship with my parents, despite the abuse. I was hoping that when they became grandparents, they would want to heal and know Eddie. My stepfather had no intention of being in Eddie's life and made it clear from the beginning. To this day, I don't think my biological father even knows I have children. My mother went through phases where one moment, she wanted to be the best grandmother ever, and the next, she didn't want to. It was the same pattern that she had with me. I wanted to believe that we could repair our relationship since I now had a child, but it was not until years later I would realize that the relationship I wanted with my mother was not possible.

During the first six months of Eddie's life, he was doing great. When he turned six months old, I noticed bruises on Eddie and did not know where they were coming from. I became very concerned and took Eddie to the pediatrician. We did blood tests and confirmed that Eddie had hemophilia. At that time, I had no idea what hemophilia was or the effect it had on the body. I did everything I could to educate myself. For a short time, Eddie was a patient up at Loma Linda. The doctor he was assigned to was wonderful, but his nurse was downright cruel. For weeks she refused to return my calls to schedule an appointment for Eddie. His pediatrician was upset with me for not understanding that I was trying to get him in. I had to file a grievance just to get him an appointment. The pediatric hematologist and pediatrician were furious with me until I explained what was going on. The following week we were seen by the pediatric hematologist, who wanted to do further testing to confirm the diagnosis. We had the testing done, and the nurse again refused to communicate. I finally, after fighting with the staff, got her to the phone. She told me the test results were in, and she would not go over anything on the phone; I had to schedule an appointment with the doctor. When I asked her when we could get in, her reply was, "Well, I don't know, maybe two or three weeks." I made it clear I was not waiting that long for serious test results. She got nasty with me and replied, "Well, he is the specialist, and he doesn't have to tell you anything." At this point, I lost it and went off on her. I replied, "And I am the mother; this is my son, and I want to know what the hell is going on! Put him on the phone now!"

She went and got the doctor, and when he answered, he explained that he was not comfortable with giving test results over the phone. I told him what the nurse did and why I was so upset. He realized that I needed to know at least where things were going. He confirmed that Eddie had hemophilia and wanted to see us in order to put a care plan together. He wanted to talk about it in more detail together. I thanked him for being honest with me and letting me know what we were going to be facing.

Tobias and I met with the doctor and worked with him for some time. I was uncomfortable, though, because I felt I could not trust the nurse and that if something bad happened to Eddie due to her reckless behavior, it could cost Eddie his life. We decided to transfer Eddie to Children's Hospital of Los Angeles. We were happy with the team that was up there and felt that they could provide the care that Eddie needed. Little did we know that, in time, we were going to have challenges that I never thought I would face in this healthcare system.

Two years after giving birth to Eddie, our son Anthony was born on January 29, 2014. Two days after Anthony was born, he was showing signs of hemophilia. When having his baby pictures done, the band-aid on his heel from the heel prick came off. It took almost ten minutes to get it to stop bleeding. The doctors told me at this point that we should wait until we do any blood tests to confirm his diagnosis. At ten months old, Tony was diagnosed with hemophilia. Due to this, Tobias and I decided not to have any more children because of what we saw our sons going through with their condition. The doctor wanted to put Tony into a clinical trial for a new medication. At first, Tobias and I were considering it. When we were presented with the agreement, it had a lot of loopholes. It pretty much summed up the fact that they would pay for our gas to take Tony to the hospital for treatment. If something happened and it severely impaired him or killed him, we would waive liability. I wanted to make sure that I was reading this correctly and that I was not overreacting as a parent. I spoke to the nurse practitioner that worked under the hematologist. I asked her, "What if my son develops an inhibitor from this?" Her answer was, "We'll discuss it at the time if it does happen." That put me in a really uncomfortable spot. I then asked her what they would do if this treatment killed Tony. Her response was the same exact thing, "We'll discuss it at the time if it does happen." I became angry and said, "No, we talk about it now, or my son is not taking part." The nurse practitioner removed him from the program, and the hematologist was furious with me. He was upset because the pharmaceutical company was going to supply the medication, so why wouldn't I allow him to take part? I told him it was due to the contract and the responses his nurse practitioner gave me. After that, he refused to meet with us and assigned my sons to the nurse practitioner, even though he knew Tobias and I didn't want that. He was determined to punish me for saying no to him. What he didn't think about was he wasn't punishing me but my sons for pushing them off onto a nurse who was not organized and thought too highly of herself.

Over the next few years of dealing with Eddie and Tony's health really had an impact on Tobias and me. We were very lucky that our insurance company covered the cost of their prophylactic treatment and supplies. It would have easily put us into bankruptcy if we didn't have the coverage we do.

Emotionally and mentally, it was draining having to inject our sons three times a week. At that time, both boys were on Advate, a prophylactic treatment used to treat severe type A hemophilia. Both boys had a port on the right side of their upper chest. We had to push a Huber needle into their chest, flush the port with saline, administer the treatment, flush the port again, and then push heparin through the port to prevent any clots. This was challenging for me, having a phobia of needles, but I had to focus on caring for my sons. The HMO would not cover the cost of a home nurse coming out, and for the two weeks we had one come out, we pretty much had around three days of training to learn how to administer such an important medication. To me, it showed the dysfunction of the American healthcare system and how little patients are thought of, and the focus being more on profit. Eddie was doing well on his treatment, but we started to see Tony was having complications. He had a joint bleed in his ankle. He had soft tissue bleeds in the past in his hand, but this was something different. I emailed the nurse practitioner and sent her pictures of Tony's ankle. I was told to monitor it. I continued to follow treatment, and it took over two weeks for Tony to heal. While experiencing his bleed, he lost the ability to walk due to the pressure. Trying to keep a toddler sitting down and keep pressure off of his foot is nearly impossible. Not long after Tony healed, the same thing happened again. Again, I got the same advice from the nurse practitioner to keep sending her pictures and monitoring it. As a parent, I thought I was doing the right thing, following and complying with orders. As this was taking place, the hematologist was not communicating with us; deep down, I don't think the nurse was communicating with him. I feared something bad was going on, and it was going to get worse.

Seeing that my sons were battling a severe and rare condition, I decided to go back for my master's in business administration to find better employment. I enrolled in a two-year program at the University of Redlands. It was a challenging program, but I was so happy to be able to learn and grow. Over time, I met a lot of great people from many different professions. I felt a lot of anxiety as a stay-at-home mother leaving me and my depression decreasing. It was so relieving to be able to work with other professionals, and I realized how much I missed working. I can say that I know I was truly blessed to be at home with my sons rather than a nanny raising them. At the same time, I never realized until I became a mother how isolating it could be to be a mother and the level of dedication it took to be a great parent. I knew it was going to be a challenge to find a balance between a career and being a mother. I knew though I had to set an example for my sons and show them that women had the same capabilities as men when it comes to careers, leadership, and the chance to make a difference.

My fear regarding Tony's condition finally became a reality. In November of 2018, we had friends come into town to attend the Epilepsy Awareness Day event that takes place yearly at Disneyland. We decided to go down to Redondo Beach for dinner and to see the boats. After finishing our dinner, as we were leaving the restaurant, I noticed Tony start to limp and rub his left knee. I asked him if he was okay, and he said yes. However, his body language said no. I picked Tony up and told Tobias we had to get home. It took a couple of hours for us to get back, and when we did, we realized we had a medical emergency on our hands. Tony had a joint bleed in his knee that was so bad it went up into his leg and pinched his sciatic nerve. My son was screaming and crying as we tried to get him out of his seat and carry him into the house. I held Tony in my arms, crying, and Tobias brought me my cell phone. I called the after-hours hematologist on call and explained the situation. I was instructed to take Tony to the ER. My friend and her mother stayed at our house with Eddie as we got Tony back in the car and headed for the emergency room. As calm as I appeared on the outside, I was in a panic on the inside. As I carried Tony into the ER, it brought back memories of having to go to the hospital by ambulance and be taken into the emergency room. I do not like emergency rooms because I have experienced a lot of trauma when being in one. We did everything we could to keep Tony calm as he had bloodwork drawn and a cat scan of his leg. They confirmed the bleed and followed up with Children's Hospital of Los Angeles. The on-call hematologist requested that Tony be brought up to the hospital by ambulance. The ER team told me the ambulance would arrive around one in the morning and to do what we could to get Tony to sleep.

One in the morning came around, and nothing. Then it was two, and then three. Tobias was struggling to stay awake. I finally told him to go home and rest. He left the hospital and called me once he was home. The ambulance arrived well after four in the morning to transport Tony to CHLA. Thankfully, Tony was sound asleep as they loaded him in the ambulance, and I got in behind him. To this day, I am not sure what route the driver took, but I remember it being after five in the morning, and everyone was driving into Los Angeles for work. The person behind the ambulance had his bright lights on and was so close to the ambulance. I was so afraid that if the ambulance had to stop, we were going to get rear-ended. I told myself to stop looking out the window and making myself anxious. We arrived at CHLA, and we went up to Hematology/Oncology on the fourth floor. Any time my sons have had to be in the hospital, it has been hard to be on that floor. Most of the children up there are battling leukemia, and to see the impact chemo is having on them is heartbreaking. We finally got into a room at six-thirty in the morning. A resident came in to admit Tony. It was a struggle to answer her questions. I didn't realize it, but I started falling asleep and mumbling. The resident got angry with me, and I let her know I had been up over twenty-four hours and I was doing my best. Once things were set, I got into bed with Tony and did what I could to get some level of rest.

By eight-thirty, Tony woke up. I ordered breakfast for him, and we watched cartoons. They started Tony on prophylactic treatment every four hours to stop the bleed and break it down. The doctor came in at ten with his residence students. He came in and acted like this was a case study situation, and I was fuming inside. My son was not a case study for these students; he was a child who was in pain. I was a mother who didn't understand what was truly going on and was scared that I might lose Tony. We did some tests and found out that Tony had an inhibitor. The actions that the nurse practitioner took were reckless. Tony spent two days in the hospital recovering from his bleed. Two days after being admitted, Tony was able to stand on his feet and walk without pain. I was relieved to see him happy and moving around. We were able to go home, yet I knew the situation was not resolved. We insisted on following up with the team and got Tony into an appointment. The nurse practitioner was in her own little world, not seeing what the big deal was. The physical therapist, however, saw it in a different way. As she looked at Tony's leg, she asked me if it had happened a couple of days prior. I let her know that he was admitted and described the previous bleeds. She told me that it was not normal and that bleeds only lasted a day or two. When I let her know they were averaging ten to fourteen days, she went to get the doctor. The hematologist came in, and he looked scared. That's when I knew the nurse practitioner was not being truthful with the doctor or with us. I was furious, knowing her recklessness could have killed my son. We put a plan together to have Tony start receiving prophylactic treatment daily. When the doctor left, they had the psychologist come in to tell us about some seminars we could attend to learn more about inhibitors. We felt at that point, things were clearing up and that we could learn and move forward. It was not the case.

Treating Tony daily brought back a lot of memories of the treatment I had as a child. Even though I took pills and not injections, it reminded me of my daily routine, knowing if I missed it, it could create a serious situation. It was the same with Tony. I felt he was being robbed of his childhood, and I could tell the situation Tony was in was affecting him as well. We were all worried about Tony and whether he was going to get past this.

Tony had another ankle bleed despite him having treatment daily. He lost the ability to walk again, and this time I was not going to allow the nurse practitioner to get away with anything. I asked for Tony to be seen and for a wheelchair for us to be able to transport him. They were procrastinating getting him in and would not put in the codes for a wheelchair. I called the pediatrician, and we got approval for the chair; they just needed the codes. Again, the physical therapist would not provide them for Tony. Even the pediatrician was getting upset, not understanding why they would not help. I was getting bills sent to me for reasons I didn't know. The supervisor refused to tell me what they were for and demanded I set up a payment plan. I refused and finally told them to send me the bills or I would report them. I received the bills, and one was for tests for Tony. The other one was for Eddie, who was not seen. The psychologist that gave us the information lied and said she did a psychological examination on Eddie and billed our HMO and medical group eight hundred dollars. The HMO paid a part, but there was over five hundred dollars due on the bill, and it had not been sent to the medical group. I was so taken aback that this woman committed insurance fraud and was trying to make a profit illegally off of my son and the insurance company. I finally had enough, and we headed up to CHLA. I walked into the department with the order for the wheelchair along with the bill to show that insurance fraud had been committed. The receptionist told us we did not have an appointment. I showed her the paperwork, and she said it was canceled without telling us. I told her we needed to see the doctor, and she refused. I told her I had enough, and if they didn't get my son back there, I was calling my lawyer. She gave me this arrogant grin as if she didn't believe me, that I was bluffing. I sat down and called my attorney and told his assistant what was going on. Once she realized I was not bluffing, that I was really on the phone with the law firm, she ran and got a nurse. The nurse came out and said I was not allowed to make the call. I told her I wanted all of the parents in the room to hear me and what my son was going through so they could advocate for their kids and prevent it from happening to them. She had me step over to another room that had two offices in it. As I was talking, one of the administrators was listening to me. He broke out laughing as I explained what was going on. At that moment, I was at my breaking point. It reminded me of the doctors experimenting on me and the emotional and verbal abuse I faced from them as well as my family. I decided it was ending here; I was ready to fight at levels they had never seen before. I got off the phone with the firm and called patient relations. I told the manager that she needed to get up there for the hospital's best interests. I stepped out of the room and saw the hematologist coming towards me. He saw how angry I was, and I yelled at him to get in the room, or I was going to file a malpractice suit against him. He ran the other way, and I went back into the room and got back on the phone with patient relations. I told her I was not joking and to get up to the floor now. I hung up the phone to see security guards coming up to the department. I knew the hematologist was getting ready to arrest me and have me banned from the hospital. The patient relations representative came in, and I told her what had happened. Then I put the bills on the table and showed her the evidence of insurance fraud that had been committed. She was beyond embarrassed and knew they were in legal trouble if the situation was not resolved. I let her know that they were getting ready to arrest me. She was confused, and I let her know security was on the floor, and my guess was they were talking to the LA PD. I then turned to her and said, "Go ahead and arrest me. If that is what it takes for my son to get the healthcare he deserves, then arrest me. But I am not going out the backdoor; I don't go out anyone's back door. If you arrest me today, I'm going down the elevators, through the lobby, and out the front door for everyone to see; I'm ready." She went as pale as a ghost, letting me know she did not want anyone arrested. I told her the hematologist had other plans. She asked me what she could do to resolve the situation. I told her to go down the hall, tell him to get in the room and tell him to do his job. Things got resolved that day, and a grievance was brought against the psychologist, and she tried to justify why she was allowed to bill us. Not long after, I was told she had left her position to seek more opportunities. My gut tells me she had a choice, leave or be fired. It was a terrible situation, but sadly it had to happen to get my children the care they needed.

We have been lucky since when it comes to the boys. A new treatment came out, and the boys changed over to that. Since then, they have not had bleeds and are functioning as any able-bodied child. The one who was not functioning that way was me. I was allowing the toxicity from the past of my own experiences and relationships to continue to consume me. I was having anxiety, depression, and night terrors, and I could no longer hide from others that I was not well. I almost hit rock bottom and knew if I didn't seek help, I was heading toward committing suicide. I went into a year of intense therapy, learning how to let go and survive. There are so many other things that I went through, and as we go through the book, I'm going to explain how I had to learn how to turn those negative situations into positive ones.

As you continue to read on, I want you to keep in mind what I said at the beginning of the chapter: we all have experienced toxicity or trauma at some level. Many are afraid to face it and heal from it due to the stigma that has been placed on mental health. I am telling you from experience if you are going to reach your goals, you need to have the strength to see what is toxic in your life and how to remove it. When I was younger, I couldn't stand the phrase, 'It's all about me.' To me, it sounded narcissistic and selfish. I am here to tell you that I was wrong to a degree. In order to succeed at your personal and professional goals, you need to put yourself first. You cannot care for your family; you cannot lead your team and accomplish your dreams without taking care of yourself. As we go through each chapter, I am going to show you examples of how to achieve your goals. I want you to start writing down those goals as we go through the book and set reasonable timelines to achieve them. Create a vision board, write a journal, do what you can to allow yourself to heal, become stronger, and show the world what you are truly made of. Even though I have shared some painful stories with you, I am going to share what I have done to heal from them. Once you start the next chapter, start it with yourself in mind and the incredible journey you are going to take to make your life the best it can be.

Things to remember:

Toxicity is extremely harsh, malicious, or harmful quality. Take a step back to see where toxicity is taking place in your life. As we go through the book, start working towards removing toxicity from your life.

Trauma from the past can re-emerge at any time. The key is recognizing what is taking place and focusing on healing. There is no shame in seeking help if you need it.

Third and most importantly, you matter. Put any negativity you have behind you, and as you face this journey, remind yourself that this is about you. You deserve to be happy, healthy, and successful.

Resources

Merriam-Webster (2022). Definition of toxicity. Merriam-Webster Dictionary. Retrieved from: https://www.merriam-webster.com/dictionary/toxicity

Pangilinan, J. (2021). 101 Toxic People Quotes to Stay Away from Negativity. Happier Human. Retrieved from: https://www.happierhuman.com/toxic-people-quotes/

Chapter 2

THE IMPORTANCE OF EDUCATING YOURSELF

"An investment in knowledge pays the best interest."- Benjamin Franklin

"Live as if you were to die tomorrow. Learn as if you were to live forever."- Mahatma Gandhi

"Knowledge is power. Information is liberating. Education is the premise of progress, in every society, in every family." – Kofi Annan

To get ahead in this world, it is essential that you are always doing what you can to educate yourself. Working to continuously educate yourself not only benefits you when it comes to opportunities, but it is excellent for cognitive health. Having sustained a traumatic brain injury makes things more challenging for me at times compared to the average able-bodied person. However, it is no excuse for me not to succeed in life, and no matter what challenges you are facing, there should be no exception for you as well.

Growing up, it was made clear that we were going to do well in school and that there was no exception; we were expected to go to college. My stepfather's mother, who I became very close to, shared her stories with me about her father leaving Lebanon at the fall of the Ottoman Empire, near the end of the first world war. She was one of the few relatives of my stepfather who I truly felt was family to me and, in my heart, will always be my grandmother. Her father had to flee the area because they were living in a Christian community, and the Turks were coming into the areas in Lebanon and Syria looking for young Christian boys to be soldiers for them instead of their children. He fled to what was British Palestine then (now Israel) and worked for a vendor in the market for three years before immigrating to America. In Syracuse, he built a small grocery store and, in time, invested in real estate. He made sure that my grandmother and her siblings all went to college due to the fact that he was unable to finish his education because of the war. My grandmother kept that tradition alive, making sure my stepfather and his siblings also obtained a higher education.

When I was younger, as much as I enjoyed learning, I felt my father made it more of a chore than a positive experience. As a mother myself now, I help my children with their work as needed and challenge them to go further than what is expected of them. I know that in this world today, it is essential for our younger generation to establish good study habits and a good work ethic in order to go on to higher education and succeed. I have seen too many who do not take things seriously and then are frustrated when they do not reach their goals.

Many people are afraid to set goals, but it is something that helps us to achieve what we want, build self-confidence, self-esteem, and build character. One thing that will help you is setting reasonable short and long-term goals. When I was working on my master's in business administration, I decided for my capstone to focus on strategic planning. I realized in taking this course how much more I had to learn. It was a course where my team and I were creating chips for automotive computers. We had to plan when we were going to release our product, the cost of research and development, what our forecast was to set a price, labor costs, and financing. During the first three weeks of the class, I felt like I was losing my mind; I wanted more than anything just to finish the class and graduate. Once I relaxed and understood the program, I realized what an awesome program it was, and I could apply it to many things, not just for-profit businesses. It has been one of the tools I have used in my nonprofit organization.

One service that I offer to people with epilepsy is college scholarships. I want to see others who are battling epilepsy achieve their dreams. Launching my organization in July 2020, in the middle of the pandemic, I knew I couldn't offer much. I was determined, though, to start somewhere. For the first two years, I have awarded two five-hundred-dollar scholarships. The winners have the option to use it towards their tuition, get an Amazon e-card for school supplies, or have it put on an Uber or Lyft account if they need transportation. It sounds like so little; many would ask how that would help anyone. Today though, you must seek every opportunity there is possible to help you reach your goals. Long-term, my goal is to be able to award five scholarships at twenty-five hundred dollars each, strictly for tuition. Because of that, I am working to create multiple sources of revenue for the foundation, so if one year we do not get a lot of grants or donations are low, there are other resources that can help us stay within our goals. Donations, monthly sponsorships, corporate sponsorships, monetization of our social media channels, CFC donations, in-person events, virtual events, and grants are the revenue resources I have developed and continue to grow, and I am working on more. If I would just rely on donations or grants, there is no way the organization would survive, and I would not be able to carry out the mission that means so much to me.

The reason for the scholarship project is that, like my grandmother, education means a lot to me as well. I reside in the United States, where higher education is not free. In order to receive a degree, you need to find grants, scholarships and take out loans. Twenty years ago, when I did my undergraduate work, it was not as challenging. You signed the loan agreement knowing that six months after you graduated, you had to start paying it back. My loan was at a 2.62 APR, and I paid $166.03 a month on a twenty-year loan. Today that is non-existent. Loans are higher in interest, you must pay them back in ten years, and the interest starts the moment you sign the papers. Imagine going through your undergraduate program, and as you are focused on studying, there is interest building on your loan, interest you cannot start paying on until you finish school.

I looked into the closest California State University, and that was California State University, San Bernardino. The annual tuition for an in-state student is $5742.00 (Cal State San Bernardino, 2020). According to Education Data Initiative, the average rate for new undergraduate loans is 3.73 percent (Education Data Initiative, 2022). Now, that might not seem like much of a jump compared to what I was charged, but remember, my interest did not start until six months after I graduated. Now, the moment you sign the agreement, the interest starts.

Here is a breakdown of costs to go to Cal State San Bernardino (tuition only, not including books, supplies, fees, or dorm costs)

1st year- 5742.00*3.73 APR= 5742.00*0.0373-= (5472+214.18= 5956.18

2nd year- 5956.18+5742= 11,698.18*0.0373 (11968.18+436.34) = 12,404.52

3rd year- 12,404.52+5742= 18,146.52*0.0373= (18,146.52+ 676.87) = 18, 822.39

4th year- 18,822.39+5742= 24564.39*0.0373= (24,564.39+ 916.25) = 25,480.64

I chose this university as an example because this is the school most students in my area apply to due to limited income. If you want the private college experience, Pomona College, which is one of the prestigious Claremont Colleges not far from me, now it is a totally different ballgame. Listed below are the costs if you want to attend Pomona College (remember this is an undergraduate degree):

Pomona College 2021-2022 Academic Year (cost of attendance for one year)

Item	On Campus	Off Campus	At Home
Tuition	$56,284	$56,284	$56,284
Fees	$402	$402	$402
Room and Board	$18,524	$15,678*	$9,316*
Books and Supplies	$1,100	$1,100	$1,100
Personal Expenses	$1500	$1500	$1500
Medical Insurance	$2782**	$2782**	$2782**
Total	$80, 592	$77,746	$71,384

*Students living off-campus are not billed for room and board. This is the average expense for living off campus or at home.

** Estimated Medical Insurance costs which are required unless a student can verify they are already covered by comparable coverage determined by the Dean of Students Office.

Source: https://www.pomona.edu/financial-aid/cost-attendance

Many students seek private schools because they want to have a good academic institution on their resume. They feel it will increase their chances of getting gainful employment, and they will have a more positive experience. That can be the experience in some situations, but it is not in all situations. Unless you have great connections, you're related to someone in a high political or corporate position, structure your resume just right, or go up and beyond to show you know what you want, going to a certain school is not going to guarantee you anything. Unless your parents or family are financially well off and can buy your way through school and into gainful employment, this is a journey for which you are going to be responsible. If you don't do your homework and make reasonable and realistic choices, in the long run, your degree can be just a piece of paper on a wall while you are working a little higher than a minimum wage job. Now imagine if you assumed just the name of a college could get you the right interview and job. Let's see how much it would be to go to Pomona College:

1st year- 80,592*0.0373= (80,592+3,006.08) = 83,598.08

2nd year- 83,598.08+80,592= 164,190.08*0.0373= (164,190.08+ 6124.29) = 170,314.37

3rd year- 170,314.37+80592= 250,906.37*0.0373= (250,906.37+ 9,358.81) = 260,265.18

4th year- 260,265.18+80592= 340,857.18*0.0373= (340,857.18+12,713.97) = 353,571.15

I don't know about you, but the thought of paying almost $354,000 for a four-year undergraduate degree is downright insane. My husband obtained his doctorate in dental surgery from the University of Buffalo for $100,000 dollars. The reason I am showing you the difference between the two is this; you must set realistic goals if you are going to succeed. If you cannot afford the private college experience, then don't go that route. I think everyone would love to have a prestigious college on their application or be able to say they went to Harvard or Princeton. I would have loved to have gone over to Europe for a year and done an overseas study, but it was not realistic with my health at the time. I'm sure no one wants to live with their parents for the rest of their lives due to student loans, but many students are doing just that here in America. Many cannot afford to pay a student loan plus pay rent and utilities.

I have had many friends start at a community college level and then go on to a university for their bachelor's and still get into a good graduate school. A few of my friends who are professors with masters and PhDs did not go to an Ivy League school. It was the hard work they did, the extra-curricular activities they did, and the volunteer or research work they did that got them through the door. They had to show that they could stand out from the average student. That's your goal as you go through this book; to set goals personally and professionally and work towards standing out from the average person and have others see the potential and capabilities you have.

Perhaps you are just starting an education or going back for higher education; research to see if the profession you want to go in has a good hiring rate, what is the average income, are good benefits involved, and what are the demographics for these careers? For years now, STEM careers and nursing have been at the top of the list. For a long time, we have had a shortage in many professions, some due to the challenges of obtaining a degree and also due to the level of stress in the profession. The challenge facing STEM professions is that you must have good critical thinking skills, can problem solve, work with data, and manage systems. Careers in engineering, computer science, math, and science are in demand and have been for years.

Nursing is another profession that is in high demand. While not as academically challenging as an engineer, it is a very stressful job and is one of the most challenging undergraduate degrees. The article, *The (Not So) Great Escape: Why New Nurses are Leaving the Profession*, discusses that due to risk of injury, being understaffed, toxic culture, and emotional strain on new nurses are having a negative impact. The main reason for nurses ending their careers is burnout from the pandemic. Despite bonuses being offered at high rates, many hospitals are still understaffed. The job stays high in demand due to as many as thirty-three percent of nurses leaving the profession within the first two years and many leaving the profession within five years (Bucceri Androus, 2021).

Humanities is an area that is often overlooked, with many assuming that the pay won't be there. Humanities has its place, though. When I was pursuing my law degree before my epilepsy took a turn for the worse, I was advised to seek a degree such as Liberal Studies, English, or History. The reason for these suggestions is they are some of the easier degrees to pursue, and your focus in getting into law school is to have a high GPA and a good LSAT. Today it takes even more, but twenty years ago, as long as you did good on your entrance exam and had a great GPA, professional schools were focused on that. Today you need so many hours of volunteering; if you are pursuing medicine or dentistry, you need to do more —

such as shadowing physicians, being a research assistant, and volunteering.

There is a place for all degrees; it comes down to what you are going to use them for and how far you really want to go. I know people who didn't want to go to graduate school at first, so they got a bachelor's degree in business, worked a while, and then pursued an MBA to move up in the company they were with. It comes down to doing your homework. What do you have a passion for, and can you realistically make a good living from it? What is the cost depending on where you want to go? Will it provide the resources you need to find gainful employment? Is it an area where you can establish a good career long-term, or are you at risk of falling out of that passion and walking away? Keep all of these in mind.

For those who cannot afford a four-year or graduate degree or have limitations that prevent them from going on to higher education, there are options to still establish a good career. After finishing my MBA, I worked as a research assistant for a professor at the University of Redlands, helping him gather data for a project. With the cost of tuition going up and a decrease in professionals such as electricians, welders, and other trade workers, researchers are working to show the importance and benefits of these careers.

CTE, or Career and Technical Education, was known as Vocational Education, which the American Government started investing in as early as 1914. For decades, the federal government invested in vocational education in high school to help students gain knowledge and skills to enter the workforce. In 1917 the Smith-Hughes Act was passed, and there was a great increase in enrollment for programs such as agriculture, home economics, trade, and industry. The bad thing about the Smith-Hughes Act was the segregation when it came to curriculum, students, and professional development, which would not be addressed until the Vocational Education Act of 1963.

In 1963, the Vocational Education Act allowed individuals from lower socioeconomic status to individuals having certain handicaps to take part in vocational education. It was amended in 1968 and then in 1976. This was important because it was now giving those who could not afford to go to college or had a disability limiting them to what type of work they could do to now being able to contribute to society. In 1984, The Perkins Act was put into place by the Reagan Administration to "expand, improve, modernize, and develop quality vocational education programs in order to meet the needs of the nation's existing and future workforce and marketable skills and to improve productivity and promote economic growth" (Friedel, 2011).

Vocational education has played an important role in American society, helping those with lower socioeconomic status or certain physical and developmental disabilities to be able to learn and find gainful employment. What destroyed vocational education in America is that it got labeled as programs for people who are poor or disabled. The result was not only having a shortage of vocational professionals such as welders, electricians, and plumbers, but it set America up for the college debt crisis.

In 2003, the year before the most current Perkins Act, Perkins III, was due to expire, the Bush Administration was set on ending all funds to vocational training. Bush's argument was that 'career and technical education had failed to demonstrate its effectiveness in improving academic achievement of high school students' (Friedel, 2011). This was far from the truth. In the article, *The Benefits of High School Career and Technical Education (CTE) for Youth with Learning Disabilities*, research from the 1980s and 1990s demonstrated that students who completed three or more years of CTE courses had a 90% completion rate compared to 72% of high school students overall. Students with disabilities, particularly learning disabilities, had lower dropout rates when taking part in CTE courses. (Wagner, et al., 2016). Luckily, there was a bi-partisan effort from both parties, and funding was not cut. Perkins IV was established and set to run until 2012. Vocational training was now going to be known as Career and Technical Education due to the advances in many of these trades.

Despite the advancement of many of these programs, students were encouraged to go to college and focus on higher education. Due to *No Child Left Behind*, many were in a situation in which they were not ready for college. The reason for this is that *No Child Left Behind* focuses strictly on test-taking. The higher the scores at schools, the more funding they get. The result is the students who are good test takers are focused on, and students who do not do as well, particularly in lower-income areas, are ignored. Creative skills such as music and art have been cut from some schools.

Assignments that require critical thinking skills have decreased. Writing skills have diminished over the years. The result is students being pushed through a system like robots focusing on the score of their tests and not so much on what they need to learn. The results of this are clearly seen in the higher academic system as students enter college in both undergraduate and graduate programs. The first year my husband started teaching at university, he gave a quiz to his students. It was a case study in which they had to diagnose what the patient had, what treatment plan they were going to put into place, and did they have to see a specialist to resolve the problem. He requested that they write it in essay form. Out of seventy students, only three knew how to write an essay; the other sixty-seven used bullet points to list the information. Because they did not follow directions, the sixty-seven who did not write an essay failed the quiz. The result? The students went to the board of the dental school to bring action against my husband, hoping he would be terminated. My husband had to go in front of the board and explain his actions and the students addressed their concerns to the board. The president of the class clearly stated in front of everyone that they did not think they were going to get graduate-level work. The academic dean of the dental school reminded them that they were in a graduate-level program and that they were going to have "doctor" in front of their name when done, so what did they think they were going to get?

It is situations like this that show that not everyone is made for college, even the ones that are great test takers on multiple choice questions. It is one thing to be book smart, but if you cannot apply your knowledge, if you cannot problem solve or critically think, you will run into trouble. It is why we all must set goals that we know are within reason. Many people, though, have been pressured into going to college despite not having the guidance or skills to reach their goals. The result is having a massive amount of debt. The reason for this is what you learn in college and what is needed in the workforce are two different things. When I started college, working on my associate's degree to become a paralegal, I learned a lot about the law, doing research, and preparing certain documents. However, when I went looking for a job, the options were very limited. Not because I was not ready, willing, or able to work but because I lacked experience. In the article, *The U.S. Education System Isn't Giving Students What Employers Need;* the author points out that the U.S. education system is not making sure that students are properly equipped with the skills and capabilities to prepare for a career where they can obtain financial stability (Hansen, 2021). It was happening twenty years ago when I entered the workforce, and it is continuing to happen now. To make things worse, the stigma that I discussed earlier regarding career and technical education is still having a negative impact on our economy. In the United States, around two-thirds of the positions available require a bachelor's or associate degree, yet many H.R. leaders admitted to tossing out resumes without four-year degrees, despite the person being qualified for the position (Hansen, 2021).

One way to gain experience is through internships while pursuing your degree. There are many paid and unpaid internships. Some people argue that there should not be unpaid internships and that it is mistreatment of students, a form of slavery. I am the first to disagree with that. Any internship I did was unpaid, but it put me in an environment where I was around professionals seeing what their job required. I could ask questions and learn from people with experience. It was hard work, but it showed potential future employers on my resume that I was making an effort to learn while pursuing my degree. I have a number of interns at my organization. Due to the small amount of funding coming in, I cannot afford to pay them. I don't even pay myself; it is a gift to my community that I am working to make a difference for.

What I do for my interns, however, is offering free mentoring to them. When preparing for a career, not many college students have mentors they can reach out to that can help them prepare for graduate programs or gainful employment. I meet with my interns to see what their goals are. I review their resumes and help them find strengths and weaknesses. I help them to build LinkedIn pages and educate them on the importance of networking, not just when they are getting ready to find work but from the moment they start working on their goals. Since launching my foundation, I have had three students complete their capstones under me. Two were accepted into the graduate psychology programs they wanted to get into; the other is taking some extra courses and preparing for her MCAT.

Having a mentor can be very rewarding. When working on my master's degree, there was a mentorship program at the university. I took full advantage of the situation and signed up to be in it. It didn't matter to me that I was working on my degree online. The fact that it was available, I was going for it. I met my mentor, who completed his MBA at the school years prior. His family had a farm in the area and owned other farms throughout the state. Within a very short time, we became great friends. He grew up in Cleveland, Ohio, about three hours from Buffalo, where I lived. The culture is very similar in both cities, and we shared lots of great stories with one another.

The best and most important thing that came out of my internship was establishing trust with my mentor. Establishing trust is essential in helping you gain something out of your mentorship. When a leader sees that you not only have the knowledge to work towards a goal but are ready to go out of your comfort zone to reach your goal, they see potential in you. Working with a mentor, whether it is focused on your career or you personally, can greatly benefit you. According to the University of North Carolina Center for Faculty Excellence, here are the benefits of working with a mentor:

Encouragement and support for growth and improvement

Guidance/collaboration in research

Teaching advice

Building a professional network

Help in becoming a leader

Receiving useful feedback on behavior

Receiving guidance on promotion and tenure

All of these benefits can help to grow a career, become a more confident professional, connect to the right people, and more. There are many ways to find a coach at a reasonable price. There are organizations that offer low-cost coaching services to help professionals grow. I have had the honor to take part in one that focuses on helping women gain strength to grow their careers and care for themselves. Many can be found on LinkedIn, and even just Googling mentor programs, you can find a number on the Google site for college students and professionals. The best thing to do is do your homework, don't expect others to do it. Take control of your goals and find the resources that will make them possible.

Along with having academic skills, interpersonal skills are a must. Interpersonal skills are the behaviors and tactics that a person uses to interact with others effectively (Tarver, 2021). While some people are natural extroverts and can easily socialize, many people have a challenge interacting with others. I will be the first to admit it has taken a lot for me to come out of my shell and socialize with others. While battling epilepsy as a child, my parents isolated me from many people. To have to go from being isolated for years to needing to socialize and work with others was overwhelming. It has taken me years to learn to socialize, and even now, I get anxious if there are a lot of people around. There are times I must do everything to focus on looking at people when talking to them. At times, I get anxious and look down, but I remind myself to relax and not to be afraid to talk to others, to focus on the conversation and not to allow fear to take over. Slowly I have gotten better, but I always make it a goal to become stronger. I have especially started to work on it now that I am in a leadership position, and I have others relying on me to set a positive example and grow our organization.

It is important to work on strengthening your interpersonal skills because it is something that employers are looking for. Are you able to communicate well with a team? If a dispute arises, how well can you handle it? Do you have the ability to collaborate with others? Can you create a healthy climate when leading a team? These may seem like simple questions, but there are many people who lack good communication skills, resulting in mistakes being made. Many are afraid to resolve a dispute. There are people who cannot collaborate and create lasting professional relationships. There are many leaders who create toxic work environments by micromanaging their workers. The results can be devastating such as a high turnover rate, missed opportunities to bring in more revenue and grow, and the inability to strategically plan and create better opportunities.

Listed below are examples of interpersonal skills that can set you apart from the average person. The goal is to do just that; stand out and have others see why they would want you for the job, why you are the one who can carry out the mission of their company.

Examples of Interpersonal Skills:

Building and establishing trust

Caring about other people

Collaborating and working well with others

Clear communication skills

Conflict management and resolution skills

Empathy

Encouraging people to do their best

Humor

Inspire others to achieve greatness

Listen to your colleagues

Mentor those under you, help them to gain new skills

Network and build professional relationships

Public speaking

Respect and sensitivity towards others, no matter who they are

Resource: https://corporatefinanceinstitute.com/resources/careers/soft-skills/ interpersonal-skills/

Most people would look at the list above and wonder why that would be so challenging in the workforce. It is because we all have different personalities, different ways of thinking, and different life experiences. The goal is to accept those differences and come together as a team. Many people do not have the capability to do that, which is a way for you to gain strength, skills, and stand out from the crowd.

I took part in an organizational leadership certification program when I finished my MBA. The vice president of the nonprofit organization I founded was already certified and encouraged me to take the courses so I could apply the knowledge as we grew the foundation. One thing that I loved about the certification was that they pointed out that at times in our lives, both personally and professionally, we will all feel vulnerable. Growing up, I was taught that feeling vulnerable was a bad thing, and that if people sensed it, they would take full advantage of you. Being vulnerable could lead you to fail, and my father told us that failure was not an option.

Failure is not the horrible thing that society has made it out to be. In fact, failure happens for us to learn from our mistakes. If we keep repeating those mistakes, then obviously, it is a bad thing. The goal is not to repeat them but to learn from them and come out stronger. An experience I had that left me feeling vulnerable happened when I first launched my organization. I was assigned to work with a mentor through SCORE, an organization that helps small business owners learn and set the goals they want for their company. The mentor reviewed the mission and vision of our organization and what we wanted to do. She flat out told me in a zoom meeting, 'there is no reason for you to even exist.' If that is not a punch to the gut, I don't know what is. I did everything I could to establish evidence for our existence, from showing we were offering services that the larger organizations do not offer to the fact that I was living with epilepsy and many of the leaders of the national organization not only do not have epilepsy, but they also really do not understand the impact it has on someone's life. She was determined to discourage me from moving forward. I took a step back one afternoon and thought about it. Was she right? Was it realistic for an organization like mine to exist?

As a strategic planner, when I come into situations like this, the way I explain it to other leaders is this: as we go down our career path, our journey, at times, it feels like we are moving ahead, and things are fine. Then we hit a bump in the road, and when we hit that bump, the path splits into two. We now must face the decision of which path we have to take. That is exactly where I was when I thought about the negative comments the mentor made to me. Do I allow her toxicity to take over and give up, or do I brush off her toxicity and keep focused on my mission and vision? I brushed her toxicity off and moved forward with my work. I stopped working with her and focused on the goals we had set for the first year. We worked hard to put our business plan into place and started getting what we needed in order to operate at the level we wanted. At the end of 2020, we finished with a profit of a little more than one thousand dollars. That comes off as a tiny amount, but the fact that we came out ahead and not in the red, especially since we launched in the middle of a pandemic, was a first victory for us. In 2021, we finished with a profit of just under seventy-five hundred dollars. It showed that our organization did have a reason to exist. We awarded two college students each a scholarship, we created our website and blog, we launched our social media, which got the word out about our mission, we started working on two additional programs we wanted to launch in time, brought in a number of interns to help, and we worked to create a strong board. That is what happens when you take a step back and allow yourself to feel vulnerable. Rather than giving up when I was told to and declaring failure, I took the risk and decided to figure it out for myself. The result has been even though we are a small foundation; we are slowly gaining ground and making a difference. Will it come overnight? No. It can take years before we reach our long-term goal. In fact, I can still fail. That is the risk when running a business. You cannot allow fear to take over, or you will fail.

To prevent setting yourself up for failure, you need to take the necessary steps to overcome the fear of failure. In the article, *How to Overcome Your Fear of Failure*, the author lists four steps to take to reduce your fears and look at the challenges you are facing, such as getting a position you want.

The first one, redefining failure, is very important to me. The Cambridge Dictionary defines failure as the fact of someone or something not succeeding (Cambridge.org, n.d.). Looking at the definition and what we have discussed about success, it shows that toxicity can come from that definition. It is easy to look at that and say, "I didn't reach my goal. That makes me a failure." The goal is to look at the situation and face it in a positive way. Maybe the goal you set was not realistic. For example, you see these ads for quick weight loss — how someone lost forty pounds within weeks using a product. Short-term, losing weight is great. Long-term, it will go right back on and then some because the goal was not realistic. Professionals recommend that the average goal for weight loss to keep it off is half a pound to a pound per week. Counting macros, avoiding processed foods, finding out if you are allergic to something, or have a hormonal imbalance, taking these into consideration can help you to create a realistic goal. It may take longer, but you increase the chances of succeeding at that goal. Impulsive acts and trying to get quick results backfire the majority of the time.

Applying for a job that you do not have enough experience for or lack the education to perform the duties, of course, your application will be rejected. It does not make you a failure. You have to say to yourself, "What can I do to make this goal possible?". If you are trying to get a promotion, is there any certification training to help with the requirements? Should you try for a different position first and then work your way to the position you want? Do you need to connect to others that work in that area? Would working with a career coach put you on the right path? It is the same thing with personal and educational goals. Do not expect things to come easily and quickly to you. Setting short-term and long-term goals is going to be the way to go.

The second, setting approach goals and not avoidance goals, is essential if you are working towards success. If you do not reach your goal the first time, step back and find out why. Approach the situation and see what happened to produce the negative result. When we fail at a goal, many feel uncomfortable, disappointed, frustrated and do not want to experience those emotions. They are difficult to deal with, but you cannot allow them to consume you. The moment you do, you are heading towards avoidance, and the chance that you will try to fulfill your goal will greatly diminish. As I mentioned in redefining failure, find out what will increase your chances of achieving that goal. Make a list and set a date on which to achieve what you need to be ready to try again.

Creating a list of what you fear and the result of that fear can help you to overcome it and achieve success. When it comes to my own fears, on and off, I have been afraid that I will fail at growing my organization and have to dissolve my nonprofit. Three months after we launched, I got Covid. I went to the hospital because my symptoms were bad, but they dismissed it as a bad cold. I caught a bacterial infection at the hospital, and for eight weeks, I thought I was fighting Covid, but I was in a lot worse shape. At the eight-week mark, my brain fog was so bad, that I could not remember how to write. I contacted my primary doctor, who put me in contact with the state Covid team. The doctor, thank goodness, figured out what was wrong with me and put me on high antibiotics for ten days. He saved my life, but the months ahead were very difficult. I had some simple partial seizures where it felt like I had an out-of-body experience; during two of them, I lost my eyesight for a short time. I was chronically exhausted, and where I wanted to be with the foundation and where I was, were at two different levels. I felt weak and was concerned I would not be able to fulfill my duties. I had to seek help and brought on a board member to help with grants as well as an accountant to help with the books. It freed up a great deal of time for me. Bringing on help and trusting others has helped me focus on getting the organization to be where it needs to be. I had to be willing to listen to others' advice and try to see things from more than one point of view.

Another fear I have is how people judge me when it comes to having epilepsy. I have cognitive impairment due to head trauma and the medications that I take. I cannot move as fast as others. Some days I have horrible fatigue; anxiety and depression are a part of my life, I have brain fog, and I must write something down, such as a meeting time, or I do not remember it. It is embarrassing when I miss a scheduled meeting or call because I forgot to put it in my phone calendar, and on my Google calendar, I don't remember it. Then someone is messaging me asking if I am still going to join. To me, it looks disorganized and unprofessional. I get embarrassed about my bad memory. I am lucky that many people I know understand the challenges that I face and know

I am not blowing them off or trying to be late. On my list, I have made a goal to slow down and make sure what I need to have on my schedule is there. I need to remember I am human, and working seven days a week as I do is challenging for someone with my health condition.

The final step is to focus on learning. I make a goal to continue to educate myself and work not just to gain knowledge but to know how to use it. Another goal is to expand my experience. I have been working with a coach on growth for my foundation as well as fundraising. Despite having an MBA, there were many things about a nonprofit that I did not really grasp. Working with a fundraising coach has helped me to find resources to use to gain supporters. Being part of a business coaching group, I have been able to ask professionals with experience what they would do or what they would expect from me for them to support my cause. The best knowledge you can get is by learning from others who have been there and done it. When it comes to our lives personally and professionally, we will never know everything or have the ability to do everything. For those who feel they can, that is a red flag. Never assume you know it all or can do it all. The end result will be failure.

Things to remember:

Education is a necessity. There are many ways to educate yourself and stay ahead.

Do the research and plan short and long-term goals to educate yourself and strengthen your skills.

Strategically plan your goals to prevent failure. Set approach goals and not avoidance goals to achieve what you are working towards.

Resources:

Barnum, M. (2017). No Child Left Behind is dead. But have states learned from it? Chalkbeat. Retrieved from: https://www.chalkbeat.org/2017/8/4/21102738/no-child-left-behind-is-dead-but-have-states-learned-from-it

Bucceri Androus, A. (2021). The (Not So) Great Escape: Why New Nurses are Leaving the Profession. Registered Nursing.org. Retrieved from:

https://www.registerednursing.org/articles/why-new-nurses-leaving-profession/

California State University San Bernardino (2022). Housing Rates and Payment Information. Cal State San Bernardino. Retrieved from:

https://www.csusb.edu/housing/getting-started/housing-rates-payment-information

Cambridge Dictionary (n.d.). Definition of failure. Cambridge Dictionary. Retrieved from:

https://dictionary.cambridge.org/us/dictionary/english/failure

Corporate Finance Institute (2022). Interpersonal Skills. CFI. Retrieved from:

https://corporatefinanceinstitute.com/resources/careers/soft-skills/interpersonal-skills/

Everyday Power (2022). Quotes About Education and the Power of Learning. Everyday Power. Retrieved from: https://everydaypower.com/quotes-about-education/

Friedel, J.N. (2011). Where Has Vocational Education Gone? American Educational History Journal, 38(1/2), 37-53.

Hansen, M. (2021). The U.S. Education System Isn't Giving Students What Employers Need. Harvard Business Review. Retrieved from: https://hbr.org/2021/05/the-u-s-education-system-isnt-giving-students-what-employers-need

Hanson, M. (2022). Average Student Loan Interest Rate in 2022. Education Data Initiative. Retrieved from: https://educationdata.org/average-student-loan-interest-rate

Kurt, D. (2021). The College Degrees You Should Have Gotten. Investopedia. Retrieved from:

https://www.investopedia.com/financial-edge/0711/the-college-degrees-you-should-have-gotten.aspx

Mensik, H. (2022). Third of nurses plan to quit their jobs by the end of 2022, survey shows. Health Care Dive. Retrieved from: https://www.healthcaredive.com/news/nurse-burnout-covid-quit-travel-incredible-health/620488/

Peppercorn, S. (2018). How to Overcome Your Fear of Failure. Harvard Business Review. Retrieved from: https://hbr.org/2018/12/how-to-overcome-your-fear-of-failure

Pomona College (2022). Cost of Attendance, 2021-22 Academic Year. Pomona College. Retrieved from: https://www.pomona.edu/financial-aid/cost-attendance

Tarver, E. (2021). Interpersonal Skills. Investopedia. Retrieved from:

https://www.investopedia.com/terms/i/interpersonal-skills.asp#:~:text=Interpersonal%20skills%20are%20the%20behaviors,listening%20to%20attitude%20and%20deportment.

University of North Carolina (2022). Benefits of Having a Mentor. University of North Carolina at Chapel Hill, Center for Faculty Excellence. Retrieved from:

https://cfe.unc.edu/mentoring/benefits-of-having-a-mentor/

Wagner, M.M., Newman, L.A., & Javitz, H.S. (2016). The Benefits of High School Career and Technical Education (CTE) for Youth with Learning Disabilities. Journal of Learning Disabilities, 49(6), 658-670.

https://doi.org/10.3102/0002831208317460

Chapter 3

PERSONAL AND PROFESSIONAL GOALS - WHY YOU NEED BOTH

"The secret of getting ahead is getting started." - Mark Twain

"If people are doubting how far you can go, go so far that you can't hear them anymore." - Michele Ruiz

"Happiness is not something ready made. It comes from your own actions." - Dalai Lama XIV

No matter where we are from, what we do for a living, or what our desires are, we all need to be able to set goals for ourselves to succeed and survive. Many people, when they hear about setting goals, get nervous, wondering if they can achieve them. Many, when they don't reach a goal, get upset and give up. The point of this chapter is that I want you to see that the goals we set cannot always be completed in a certain way by a specific time. There are goals that, for some reason, are not attainable, but it does not make you a failure because of it. Depending on what kind of goal it is will decide how long it will take and what steps you need to take to achieve your goals. The purpose is to learn how to strategically plan out your goals, what tools you need to reach your goals, and the type of environment you need to be able to reach your goals.

First and foremost, what are you hoping to achieve? That is the question to ask yourself. Do you want to spend more time with your family, take a once-in-a-lifetime trip, or learn a new skill? Do you want a promotion and to take your career to the next level? Do you need to find more balance between your personal life and professional life? Think truly about what you want to do. There are no silly questions; everything is on the table. Take the time to brainstorm and think about what is best for you and how it will affect you and those around you.

The reason I say this is because life, in general, happens, and we are not always prepared for what comes next. Even as I write this book, I'm reminding myself I must practice what I preach. I took a vacation with my family just a little over a month ago. My husband Tobias, our sons, and I flew to Germany to the village Tobias grew up in. Tobias' family lives in a village in Bavaria, not far from the Austrian border. Going over, I can't tell you how much work I took with me. I had created a folder in my email filled with information. Information on writing the book, putting together some presentations for my interns to work on, and a certification project I am putting together. It doesn't sound at all like I was planning on taking a vacation, but I was determined not to fall behind on work.

Arriving in Germany, I found out that my sister-in-law's family was staying with my in-laws. My sister-in-law Julia is originally from Ukraine and lived at times in Russia. Her mother, sister-in-law, and nieces came to Germany so the girls could continue school and get away from the violence. The internet connection was horrible, so I couldn't work during the day as the girls needed to focus on their online classes. After flying thirteen and a half hours from Los Angeles to Munich with no sleep, I was frustrated trying to figure out how I was going to get on a schedule and get a few things done.

Thankfully, the one and only meeting I scheduled went well, and I felt I could work at night and rest during the day. Jetlag had other ideas, and the more I tried to find some way to get things going, the harder it was. A few days after arriving in Germany, a bad storm came through the area. One of the things that trigger my seizures to take place is a sudden drop in barometric pressure. We were coming back from the grocery store, and I started feeling nausea and a migraine coming on. I did everything I could to stay calm; I didn't want my sons to know something was not right. I hurried into the house and got myself up to the bathroom. I got sick and had to lie down on the floor. The pressure was so bad in my head; I couldn't sit up; I had to lie there and just allow my body to decide when it would allow me to have control again. I didn't know if I was having a small seizure or a reaction to the migraine. I felt lost, confused, and not in control. I spent the rest of the day in bed, trying to sleep and recover.

The next morning, I was still not well. I started to realize that what I wanted to get done was not going to get started anytime soon. When I feel my schedule is off and that I'm not getting things done, it stresses me out. Tobias told me to relax and remember that I was there on vacation. I should have listened to my husband, but in the back of my mind, my goals, and my responsibilities, were all still there. It was the first time in twelve years that I had taken a vacation. I hadn't realized how much work had become a part of my everyday life and that I truly had forgotten how to relax and not think about what I needed to do next. I did what I could to relax and be with my family but feeling sick was preventing just that.

A few days later, Tobias and I went to Italy to join friends we hadn't seen in a few years. We were joining my alumni group and professors as well as a few students who were involved in the study abroad program. We took a train from Munich to Venice, which was beyond beautiful. To go through the mountain regions and see the changes in the landscape was amazing. What I loved, though, was as we stopped at different stations throughout Germany, Austria, and then Italy, you could feel the change in the environment and the change in culture as we got closer to Venice. When we got off the train and onto the Vaporetto, it was amazing to go around the main area to get to our hotel. I thought that what happened when I got sick was just something very brief and that everything would be fine from there. However, it ended up being the opposite. Over the next few days, I found myself having auras again and feared something was going to happen. I couldn't stay out late with friends because I truly was exhausted. I became confused one morning in the middle of San Marco Square and was not sure how I got there. It started to frighten me because I had not had any seizures in years, where I became that confused. I continued to tough things out, determined to have the perfect time with Tobias, but Tobias could clearly see my struggles. We went on to Trieste, and I continued to feel sick. I decided to increase my medication by adding an afternoon dose to prevent things from getting worse. I can tell you from living with this condition for forty-two years now I know my body better than most doctors, even though they don't want to hear that. I will say, out of respect for my neurologist, that I shouldn't have changed anything without emailing him first. Seeing how I was around 13,000 miles from him, I felt I had to do something. Thankfully it helped, and my symptoms decreased.

We were able to enjoy the city for another couple of days before heading to Ljubljana in Slovenia. When arriving, I started experiencing symptoms again. It was starting to get to me emotionally and mentally. We went back to our hotel one afternoon, and it just hit me. I felt exhausted and upset with myself, feeling I had not spent enough time with my husband and children for years. I emailed my board members, letting them know what was happening with my health. I was so frustrated; part of me wanted to dissolve my foundation. I just wanted to stop working and not feel so attached to my work. Thankfully, one of my board members Chris, who has epilepsy himself, called me. He told me, "No, you're not dissolving anything. We're going to talk about how you're feeling and how we're going to get you better." He told me how sorry he was that I was experiencing some small seizures and auras when I was supposed to be on vacation. I told him how upset I was that I had not even started on anything I had brought over to work on. He stopped me and said, "The point of going there was to have time with Tobias and the boys. Why are you even thinking about work?" I then realized how much my career became part of my life and said, "I'm just so used to working; it feels strange not to be working." That right there was the red flag that I needed to make some serious changes to my personal and professional goals. I was overworking, not balancing my family life and professional life, and due to stressing about it, I was making myself sick. It took everything in me to promise Chris that I would not open my folder and work on anything. Chris told me that my job from that point until I arrived home was to take care of myself, have quality time with my family and that I could get past what had happened. A short time later, I received emails from my other three board members telling me the same thing. It felt wonderful to know my team believed in me and would not allow me to give up. I promised all of them the same thing that I promised Chris and told them once I was home, I would follow up with them.

Listening to my team and following through on my promise was easier said than done. Anytime I thought for one second about work, I reminded myself of what I promised to do. After a few days in Slovenia, Tobias and I flew to Denmark to see our friends Stephanie and Annis. They live not too far from Billund, where LEGOs were invented. One of my passions is building LEGOs. When I was young, and my seizures were not well controlled, the happiest times I had by myself were building LEGO cities. I had a couple of buckets filled with LEGOs, and being creative really helped to get my mind off the challenges I was facing. Even now, at forty-four, I still buy sets at times, build them, and display them in my office. I love the Star Wars Collectibles as well as the Creator Expert buildings.

We went to the LEGO House and visited the museum. We saw lots of displays and took part in some of the activities. At one point, Tobias and I sat down at one of the stations to build bumblebees out of LEGOS and put them on display with the other ones many children built with their parents. In the past, I would have judged myself and thought how silly it must be for a grown woman to be still playing with building blocks. At that point, though, I didn't care. I decided one of my personal goals was to find myself again. Not the Natalie that worked all the time, but the Natalie who would start enjoying life again, do the things she loved, and have time with the ones she loved.

We met up with Stephanie and Annis and had a wonderful time together. We went to Legoland, ate at some great restaurants, went on a hike, and just had quality time together. Spending time with my friends and not just talking on Facebook Messenger was so uplifting. We stayed at a bed and breakfast and made dinner, and had a wonderful meal one evening. The owners of the bed and breakfast owned a piece of land and had two ponies there. Tobias and I went to the grocery store and got apples and carrots for the ponies. We spent our last morning there feeding the ponies and having the time of our lives. At that point, what I needed to do happened; I pushed work out of my mind and focused on making sure the last days of vacation were special.

We flew back to Munich and joined my in-laws again. I was so happy to see my sons had a great time bonding with their grandparents and experiencing a totally different culture. Both of my sons told me they wanted to move to Europe to be closer to their grandparents. At this point, I don't know if it was possible if Tobias and my careers could make that happen. I told the boys we would consider it and work towards getting closer to family. My in-laws were so happy with how well-behaved the boys were that they invited them to visit next summer. My sons were overjoyed, and Tobias and I told them they had to learn to give one another their medication while there. They must inject their medication every two weeks. I told them I wanted them to work on their German to improve their speaking skills to reduce the language barrier. My in-laws speak broken English, and it is very challenging at times fo them to understand English now that they no longer travel and don't hear it. Both of my sons agreed they would work towards their two goals so they could go back and be with family.

Coming home was sad for all of us, yet we had to get back to our normal routine. Arriving home, I decided it was time to focus on my goals and what I was going to do to gain a better work-life balance.

When it comes to setting goals, you want to remind yourself of what you are working towards. It is very easy to get back into old habits and not follow through. I'm going to go into some examples of tools you can use to keep track of your goals. Keep in mind what works for one person may not work for another. Do some research and find something you feel connected to that will help you and encourage you to accomplish what you set out for.

One of my favorite tools to use for keeping track of my goals is journaling. You can create a journal in many ways, from a simple notebook to typing it up on Microsoft Word to using a journal app or goal-setting software. Pick what you feel most comfortable with; this is about you. I like to write everything down, so I prefer a simple black-and-white composition notebook you can get at the store. You can also buy a diary and have it be something special that only you have access to. My mentor, who I worked with when pursuing my master's, has a whiteboard where he has three personal and three professional goals written. He hung the whiteboard across from his bed so when he wakes up daily; it is the first thing he sees. If that works for you, do it.

Even though I am more comfortable writing, I decided to take a different route in planning my personal and professional goals. I saw numerous reviews on journal apps that were positive and decided to give it a try. I selected one and decided to try it out. Because I was determined to change my habits after what happened on my vacation, I decided to try something new and not fear change. I downloaded the app and first put in three personal goals:

- Walk a minimum of 30 minutes on the treadmill daily to improve overall wellness
- Spend time daily with my children playing, watching cartoons, and having quality time together

-Eat healthy and focus on maintaining a healthy weight

I kept my first three goals quite simple. I didn't want to get too specific at this point or even go to the level of making any long-term goals. In the past, I have made the mistake of starting long-term right away instead of keeping it simple. For example, if I wanted to lose a lot of weight, in the past, I would have made a goal to lose fifty pounds. That goal wouldn't last long because it felt like I was never going to get there, and I would give up. For a goal like this, it takes a short-term and long-term approach; start short-term. Write down, "I am going to lose five pounds." To keep weight off long-term, it is best to lose half a pound to a pound a week. If you are trying to lose fifty pounds, it's going to take a year. Most people would cringe at hearing that. Five pounds, however, feels more within reach. When you reach your goal, allow yourself to celebrate your accomplishment. Then say to yourself, "I was able to lose five pounds; my goal is to lose another five." Then keep going until you reach your goal. You may hit a bump in the road, and your weight may plateau. It is not a reason to give up. Look at your situation and work to find out why suddenly you are not achieving your goal. Calculate your basic metabolic rate, and find out what your macro count should be. You might not be eating enough, and your body is holding onto everything. You might be eating certain foods that are preventing your weight loss. Taking the time to educate yourself to find a solution to the problem will increase the chances of succeeding at your goal. Remember, keep it simple.

Professional goals tend to take a more strategic approach as there are many factors to consider. Is this going to be a goal to move up in the company you are at, is it going to be a career change, or are you looking to expand your knowledge and create better opportunities for yourself? Professional goals take more than just a journal, as discussed with personal goals. In some situations, you may need to talk to your boss or a mentor to help you plan your goals to increase the chance of succeeding at them. In the article, *How to Set Professional Goals and Plan Out Your Career*, the author points out some very valid points to take into consideration that I feel you can truly benefit from.

The first and more important step is just do it. Do not wait for a mentor, supervisor, or director to suggest it. If you truly know what your desires are, if there are goals and dreams that you want to work towards, then start doing it. At the same time, you need to have goals that will cause you to act on them, be able to set a certain timeline to achieve them and have them be realistic. See where you are in your career and what you truly envision yourself doing. It's at this point you should talk to your supervisor, a mentor, professor, or someone you trust who you feel will take your goals seriously and will be ready, willing, and able to guide you in the right direction.

One tool that I have used for professional goals that I really like **is the SMART goals setup.** SMART stands for the following:

- **Specific:** Well-defined, clear, and unambiguous
- **Measurable:** with specific criteria that measure your progress toward the accomplishment of the goal
- **Achievable:** Attainable and not impossible to achieve
- **Realistic:** Within reach, realistic, and relevant to your life purpose
- **Timely:** With a clearly defined timeline, including a starting date and a target date.

(Corporate Financial Institute, 2022)

According to the Corporate Financial Institute, you need to break down these steps to truly understand how to use the technique to reach your goals. We are going to break down each one to understand how to set up your goals.

Step 1: Specific Smart Goals:

The following questions need to be considered when creating a goal:

Who is involved in the goal?

What do you want to accomplish?

Where is the goal going to be achieved?

When do you want to achieve your goal?

Why do you want to achieve the goal?

(Corporate Financial Institute, 2022)

Is it going to be primarily you when it comes to this goal, or will this be a team effort? What is it you want to accomplish and do you have the tools to do it? Where do you have to be to work on this goal, and what is your timeline? One of the most important questions I feel in the specific part is "why." Why are you doing this? It is easy to say you are just doing it for yourself, but be specific about it. Is it to gain knowledge, be happier, or have an experience not many get to have in life? Make sure you truly understand why you are setting this goal for yourself so you can succeed at it.

Step 2: Measuring your goals:

Measuring your goal is essential to be able to establish a realistic timeline in reaching your goal. Consider the following when it comes to measuring your goals:

How many goals/how much can you do?

How do you know you have reached your goal?

What is your indicator of progress?

(Corporate Financial Institute, 2022)

A perfect example here is the weight goal I brought up in the beginning of the chapter. Let's break it down here:

Goal: To lose 50 lbs. I want to feel healthier, work out at the gym, accomplish my goal in one year, and improve my overall health and well-being.

How many goals/how much can you do: There are two goals here. The first is the short-term — to lose five pounds at a time (aiming for half a pound to a pound per week). The long-term goal is to lose a total of fifty pounds.

How you know you have reached your goal: By keeping a journal and tracking your progress. Accomplishments can be weight loss, an increase in energy, and improvement in mental/emotional health.

What is my indicator of progress: Feeling happier and having more energy. Your clothes are getting looser on you. You go down a pant size and treat yourself to a new pair of jeans. You feel a boost in self-confidence knowing you are making progress.

So, using this method, you can write down the specific goal and how it will be measured:

"I will set a goal to in one year lose fifty pounds. Short-term, my goal will be set to lose five pounds at a time (a half pound to one pound per week). I will join the gym and work out four days a week for 30-60 minutes per workout, tracking my workouts and making adjustments as needed. Every Sunday, I will weigh myself to see if I am making progress. I will set rewards for myself when I achieve my goals."

As you can see, the information above is specific to what you want to do, and you are able to measure your achievements. You have set up an attainable timeline that will allow you to adjust your goal if needed, and it is realistic. If you put down that you were going to lose fifty pounds in three months, the chances of you succeeding at the goal would be little to none. If anything, you would end up making yourself very sick. By putting your body in starvation mode to quickly lose a lot of weight, you can greatly increase the chance of your injuring yourself while working out by not getting the proper nutrients your body needs to develop muscle and burn fat.

Step 3: Achievable:

The third step of the SMART system focuses on is your goal achievable or even attainable. Focus on the following when developing your goal:

Do I have the resources and capabilities to achieve this goal? If not, what am I missing?

Have others done it successfully before?

Corporate Financial Institute, 2022)

The first question is very important. Let's say your goal in this situation is to get a promotion. Next year when your contract for work renews, you want to move up and obtain a decent raise. Are the resources there, and do you have the capacity to reach this goal? What would you need to do to achieve it? When I obtained my MBA, many who were in my program were already working in the business field and wanted to move up to a mid-management position. One of my friends went to her supervisor and discussed her goals. They paid eight percent of her tuition, and she had some additional requirements to be promoted to her next position. Some companies will do that, while others will not. Can you afford to obtain an MBA? If not, what certifications can you take to help you gain the skills and expand your knowledge, helping you get closer to your goal? Not everyone is going to have access to the same tools. You need to take into consideration what resources are available to you before you can even start working towards a goal.

When it comes to success, many have accomplished great goals, whether personally or professionally. Remember, we are all human, yet we have different skills and capabilities; that's what makes us unique. My husband, Tobias, is a periodontist and has a passion for caring for people with chronic illnesses. He has helped many save their teeth through bone and gum graphs. He places implants and does sinus surgery as well. I would never set a goal to become a periodontist because I don't have the stomach for it. I can tell you over the years, when Tobias has reviewed CT scans or pictures of people's mouths, I take one look at those pictures and remind him that he's one in a million because they couldn't pay me enough to do what he does. I would fail at the goal of becoming a periodontist, yet Tobias excelled at it and reached the goal. Don't allow the success of others to make you feel like you are a failure. You have a talent, a gift; we all do. The challenge in life is finding that talent, that gift you have, and using it to your advantage. You want to aim for a goal that has been proven to be successful, yet make sure it is one you know you can obtain and don't compare yourself to others. Focus on yourself and what you are capable of.

Step 4 - Realistic Goals:

The fourth step focuses on establishing realistic goals. When setting a goal, it must be realistic. Can you physically do what you want? Do you have the emotional and mental strength to achieve the goal? Do you have the knowledge or financial means to make it happen? Are the resources you need available? Can you commit to the goal, and is it within reach? These are just some questions you must answer yourself.

For example, Jeff Bezos set a goal to have the biggest super yacht in the world. According to Bloomberg, the former CEO of Amazon's net worth is currently one hundred forty billion dollars, a number most of us on this earth can't even wrap our heads around. The yacht he is building is 127 meters in length, around 57 feet longer than a football field. The project, according to Bloomberg, is projected at 500 million dollars to build. Bezos has the financial means to reach his goal, yet at the same time, he did it, upsetting a lot of people. In the Netherlands, where his yacht is being built, the government agreed to take apart the Koningshaven Bridge, which is in one of Europe's busiest cargo ports (Walt, 2022). It is the only way to get his yacht out of the port. Many people, including local politicians, are furious that Bezos thought he could just throw money at the government to get his own way. To the people of the Netherlands, the bridge is a historical landmark, and they are very taken aback that it is going to be dismantled. In fact, an online protest was created, and according to Newsweek, as many as 4,000 people planned to throw rotten eggs at the yacht when it was going to leave the port.

The yacht was scheduled to leave port this June, but I haven't been able to find anything confirming that it has left at this point. I honestly cannot blame the locals for being upset with Bezos requesting that the bridge be taken apart. Jeff Bezos does not have the best reputation for being a loyal employer.

Forbes magazine disclosed the investigative report showing that Amazon's worker's needs were neglected. Many had their checks cut short due to pay calculations being wrong. Despite the problem being brought to their attention by many employees, Amazon continued the practice. When it comes to reputation, Amazon's looks tarnished, with a record high turnover rate for hourly employees, at 150% a year (Brancaccio et al., 2021). Amazon, however, sees this as a benefit, being able to bring in new employees at a lower pay while paying employees a bonus to leave. Most people would say, "Why does that matter? It's his money, his business." In the business world, however, reputation means everything, no matter how much money you have. To have reports coming out about people being underpaid, disability payments suddenly stopping, wrongful termination, and employee burnout leaves a very negative impact on Bezos' history at Amazon. Despite bringing in billions for the company, any image of unethical behavior can tarnish not just the person who committed the act but the company where it happened.

I know that after reading the information about Bezos, you are probably thinking, "What does that have to do with goal setting?" When you set goals for yourself, they have an impact on the people around you. It might not seem like it, but they do especially professional goals. Realistically, Bezos has the funds to have his dream super yacht. His reputation, however, shows that this was a very tasteless goal to have when his company was dealing with these issues, issues he created while leading. Make sure the goal you are working towards is realistic, that you have the means to get it done, and to make a positive impact for yourself. If you are working towards a leadership position, make it an additional goal to have a positive impact on others. Be the leader that your team can trust, that they can confide in, and know that their opinion is respected. Establish a reputation as a leader who has helped to establish a strong culture at the company, but also a positive climate for workers. In doing this, you will have a lower turnover rate, you will have loyal employees, and you will establish a positive reputation. Taking these steps can open doors and create many opportunities for you.

Step 5 – Timely:

The final step in SMART goals is time. When do you want to reach your goal, or does your goal have a deadline? The example goal that I gave with the weight loss showed how important the time factor is when setting a goal. The goal was to lose fifty pounds. Due to wanting to lose half a pound to a pound each week, we calculated that this was going to take at least a year. Because of the time it would take, it was important to establish short-term goals to help us stay focused and increase the chances of reaching the long-term goal.

When it comes to a professional goal, putting a time frame on a project or goal is important. If you want to go back to school to obtain higher education to be promoted, go through the SMART steps. What are you wanting to achieve? How much can you do? Are the resources there to go back to school? Is it a realistic goal? How long will it take? If you want to obtain a promotion, you would have to work out a schedule for classwork and studying. You will have to make sure that you can commit to such a time-consuming and expensive goal. Realistically, will spending the money, working hard, and obtaining the degree pay off long term? No one wants to spend tens of thousands of dollars only to receive a small increase in salary and then be stuck with student loans. The time you would have to spend will take away from personal time, family time, and putting things on hold that you might otherwise like to do. Will it be worth the sacrifice?

The SMART goal tool is excellent for goal setting. I like using it for professional goals and strategic planning. At the same time, you can use it for personal goals, as I demonstrated. Give it a try and create one personal goal and one professional using the SMART goal tool. You will find it will make you think critically about everything and open your eyes to possible new opportunities.

For those who like to keep things simple, tools such as a vision board are a benefit. Putting a vision board in an area that you can frequently see can be a great reminder and help you to stick to your goals. What my mentor created with the whiteboard is one example of a vision board. You can also be creative and make one on a program such as *Canva*. I made one on *Canva* as an example that focuses on a different aspect of life. There are a ton of templates, so you can pick what suits you best and helps you stay focused. Here is the one that I made:

MY VISION

BOARD

PERSONAL

I am going to go to the gym 3 times a week. Goal is to improve my physical and mental health

FAMILY

Every Sunday will be family day and I will spend the day with my kids having fun

RELATIONSHIP

Tobias and I will have a date night once a month

CAREER

In two years, I want to be involved in public speaking on a regular basis. I want to start a second book.

HEALTH

I want to improve my mental health, get better sleep, and reduce my depression.

LIFESTYLE

I want to find a balance to work and my personal life. One day out of the week I will not do any work and will do something that makes me happy.

Resource: Canva Pro

There are many resources to help with personal and professional goal setting. Find the ones that work best for you and use them. They are there to build you up, help you see your potential, and help you achieve what you might think now is unachievable.

We have established ways to set goals and carry them out. Now, what skills do we need to carry these goals out, especially in the workforce? One thing you need to take into consideration is your emotional intelligence. Mental Health America defines emotional intelligence (EI) as the ability to manage both your emotions and understand the emotions of people around you. There are five key elements of which you need to be aware: **self-awareness, self-regulation, motivation, empathy, and social skills**. All five of these key elements are important, and there are many people who lack them. Out of the five, I have found empathy really lacking in the business world. Learning how these key elements can affect your decision-making is important. It can make or break a career if someone has low emotional intelligence. Be aware of how you act in the work setting. What are you feeling, how do you come off to others, and what actions do you take? When it comes to your colleagues, it can be challenging. No one can control another person's emotions, but if someone brings toxicity into the work environment, you need to know how to deal with that toxicity and avoid being toxic yourself. When people act toxic and stir the pot in an environment, most of the time, they are in pain due to past trauma or being in a toxic environment at home. It is not an excuse to be that way; I want to make that clear. However, some people do not have the strength to seek help or may even be afraid to. This is when empathy is important. You cannot control other people's actions, but you are able to control yours. If you fight fire with fire, you're going to get burned. If you have a toxic worker on your team, avoid making impulsive decisions. Take into consideration why they may be that way, and do what you can to establish a civil and professional relationship. Motivate them to go the extra mile and show that they have the potential to carry out goals. When you show empathy towards others, over time, the toxicity can start to go down, and a healthy work climate can be established. Now it doesn't always work. Some people may not be able to change, but do the right thing and do your part. Don't contribute to the toxicity.

Social skills can be the most challenging. I will admit it is a challenge for me at times. I'm more of an introvert; I am happiest when I am at my desk doing research. Being in a leadership role, however, I have had to learn how to be around others, which at first was very difficult. Growing up with epilepsy, my parents prevented me from socializing due to being overmedicated and the challenges I had with the side effects of my medicine. I spent more time in my room by myself as a child than I did anywhere else. To go from being alone for a good part of my life to having to be in front of a crowd was very intimidating at first. I had to tell myself that if I was going to be the face of an organization, if I was going to lead, then I had to face my fears. There are still times when it takes everything in me to make eye contact. I can be talking to someone for the first time about my work, and I can just feel the anxiety flowing through me. I must tell myself to take a deep breath and focus. The challenge with social skills is when we communicate, we communicate through verbal and non-verbal actions. If someone tells you to have a nice day, but they look angry at you, you are going to focus on their non-verbal behavior. Why would they wish you a nice day when they look like you have offended them in some way? Work on balancing your verbal and non-verbal communication skills. If you ask a colleague to do something and they say yes, but look anxious, it can be several things. They may feel overwhelmed and have a lot of work already. They don't want to say no, though, fearing they might upset you. It might be a task they have never carried out, and learning something new is intimidating. Be aware of their emotions, communicate and be supportive, and let them know that it is okay to ask for help. Many fear that asking for help is a sign of weakness. I'm telling you now that is not the case. Think of it as a way to grow, to learn from others. My friend Will and I completed our strategic planning capstone together. Despite being in the same line of work, I review my strategic plan with him at times when it comes to our foundation. The reason for this is while I'm deep in work, I want to make sure I am not missing anything and that I am taking all important key factors into consideration as I set goals to establish and grow the organization. Will is very good at goal planning and is passionate about business development and organizational leadership. Knowing the organization can benefit from that passion, I would be foolish not to ask him for help at times. I may be the founder of the organization, but I cannot create, grow, lead, and manage an organization on my own. I would set myself up for failure; it is a team effort. Will is part of my team, and I know reaching out to him and getting his professional opinion is a benefit for the organization and those we are trying to help.

Another thing you need to take into consideration is social conformity. Conformity is a type of social influence involving a change in belief or behavior in order to fit in with a group (McLeod, 2016). Conformity has a large effect on employees on the job. People want to get along with their colleagues; they want to get along with their supervisors; they want to be accepted for who they are. There are different types of conformity that someone can face in the workforce.

Compliance, or group acceptance, occurs when someone is willing to act in a certain way to gain approval from the group, even if they don't agree with what they are doing. Instead of being themselves, they are willing to act in a certain way or say something to fit in with the group. Group acceptance reminds me of peer pressure when being a teenager. If you wanted to be with the popular kids, you had to follow along and do what they did to be accepted. If you didn't, you were an outsider and labeled "weird," "geeky," "lame," and many more labels. Even though we are adults now, we still fall into that situation of wanting to be accepted. There was a specialist that used to work at the university where my husband, Tobias, works. He had a very arrogant attitude and would talk down to many of the dental assistants and students. He had a reputation for being a bully. One of the general dentists I know was able to strike up a friendship with this specialist. The general dentist is a nice guy, and I consider him a friend. For years when his parents would come into town, we would meet for dinner, and they were family to us. One day when I was at the clinic, the specialist that loved to talk down to people disrespected me. The general dentist was right there and saw the entire thing. Instead of telling the specialist that he was out of line, he looked in the other direction and remained silent. The next time I saw the general dentist, he apologized to me but then said, "Well, you know how he is." He was more worried about the specialist being his friend and accepting him instead of calling out his arrogant behavior. That often happens in the workforce because no one wants to be on the bad side of a bully. He didn't agree with the negative behavior, yet at the same time said nothing.

Internalization affects us in a different way. While compliance causes us to act in a certain way in public but feel or believe something different, internalization causes changes in our behavior and how we perceive things. Many may feel the pressure to dress a certain way or style their hair a certain way for acceptance. This is known as respectability, which refers to "the set of social guidelines dictating acceptable behavior" (Gassam Asare, 2022). When people in leadership positions establish an environment where respectability takes place, it puts many employees at a disadvantage. Having to look a certain way, believe certain things, or live life a certain way should not be involved in determining who deserves to move up in the company. A lot of times, though, it does. Many people face discrimination in the workforce due to their race, gender, sexual preference, religion, ethnicity, or disability. They know the pain of working in an environment affected by respectability, a pain that should not exist.

As a woman with multiple chronic illnesses, three of them falling under the Americans with Disabilities Act, I can tell you

I have experienced being in an environment affected by respectability. Many times, professionals have spoken to me like I was a child. Projects I have worked on, where if someone able-bodied was running it, would receive positive feedback and credit for their achievement. The feedback I get, they feel it is positive, yet I find it very condescending. While an able-bodied worker might be told 'good job,' the response I tend to get is, "Why, isn't that special! You're just so inspiring!". I'm not a little four-year-old who was a good girl and got a gold star for it. I'm a forty-four-year-old woman who pays bills, cares for her family, fulfills my adult responsibilities just like any other adult. Yet, in the mind of these people, I am someone who must not be able to survive because I am "different," "diseased," and should not be allowed to have the same opportunities.

As hard as it can be, don't allow other people's toxicity and insecurities to affect you. I can tell you that just sharing what I did, brought my blood pressure up some, thinking about it again. It is very easy to take situations like that personally. Don't allow it to, you're only upsetting yourself if you do, and it will not affect those who acted in that way. I have had professionals in my community tell me how smart I come off, but they would never hire someone of my kind. One of the city councilmen in my city questioned the validity of my master's degree. He looked at my business card and saw that I had MBA after my name. He looked at me and asked, "Where did you get your master's? Just so I can verify." I told him I went to the University of Redlands, and if he would like, I was more than happy to send him a copy of my graduate transcripts. If he needed to speak to someone at the university,

I would contact the academic dean and let him know that I gave the city councilman permission to speak to him regarding my time there as a student. He stood there in shock for a second, surprised that I had stood up for myself. He then went, "Oh, okay. Thank you." Then he walked away as if the conversation had never taken place. That is just one of many examples of what I have experienced in the workforce and being an entrepreneur.

The reason for sharing those two examples was to demonstrate how stigmatization can affect the goals you are working towards. It is hard to be in an environment where there are professionals looking down on you for being different, yet you are expected to perform at the same level they do. In my case, it is due to having a neurological disorder. Having an invisible illness, I can decide who to tell and who not to tell about my health conditions. Now that I have created a nonprofit foundation advocating for those who have epilepsy, it is out there that I have epilepsy. I knew the risk I was taking in creating my foundation and that once I did, there was no going back. If I had remained silent, no one would have guessed that I have epilepsy. I would still be the worker that was reliable, a good team player, and willing to go the extra mile. That all went away when I let others know I have epilepsy. It has now been replaced with the word liability. That's all I am seen as by most professionals. There are some professionals that can see past that and enjoy working with me. A lot, however, cannot see past it and do not want to see past it.

You cannot change anyone who has negative views, but you can take their negativity and find a way to make it positive.

In the last semester of my undergrad, I had a seizure while in class one night. It was winter, and I had a horrible bronchial infection. My doctor had given me some nasal spray to help break everything up. He didn't realize that one of the chemicals in the spray was known to trigger seizures. I had a complex partial seizure, and they had to take me to the hospital by ambulance. I was out of it for a couple of days, trying to recover and get my energy back. Once I recovered, I went back to school, and the counseling center let me know that the disability director wanted to talk to me. I went to her office, and she tried to convince me to withdraw from college and not graduate. She put her hand on mine and said to me, "Honey, not everyone is college material." I pulled my hand away from hers and glared into her eyes. I felt furious that she had the audacity to say such a thing. I replied, "Well, guess what honey? I am, and I will be walking across that stage in May." I left her office and went to the academic dean and let him know I would not be bullied out of school over a seizure. Thankfully, I had his support and the support of my professors. They were not going to let me leave, knowing how much my goals meant to me. I could have very easily given in to her and left. I was determined, however, to show her that people with epilepsy have the capability to achieve goals and that we are not second-class citizens. I took her negativity toward people with disabilities and turned it into a positive by completing my classes and graduating. Walking across that stage and receiving my degree felt amazing, knowing that instead of running away from my challenges, I faced them head-on, knowing I could accomplish what I wanted.

The result of internalization and respectability is negative and can have a major impact on someone and those around them. Self-esteem can be greatly decreased and self-worth shattered. Many professionals, when experiencing this, start to question their abilities and, in time, develop imposter syndrome. In situations like this, finding a mentor or taking part in a mentorship program can be beneficial. There are many organizations that will help professionals take part in mentorship programs at a low cost. Working with a mentor or career coach can help in developing better skills, learning to advocate for yourself, and helping you to grow and thrive in the workplace.

Conflict resolution is something that all professionals need to know how to use to establish a positive climate in the workforce. Seeing the impact that social conformity and emotional intelligence can have on the workforce when things don't work out, a solution must be found to keep productivity going. Conflict resolution is defined as the informal or formal process that two or more parties use to find a peaceful solution to their dispute (Shonk, 2022). In the article, *The Top 5 Conflict Resolution Strategies for the Workplace*, the author lists five important strategies that will help you not just to resolve a situation but to create strategies and help you to learn how to avoid conflict.

The first step is not to ignore the conflict. First and foremost, if you are experiencing conflict in your workplace, the more you ignore it, the higher chance it is going to get worse. Acting passive-aggressive can result in tensions increasing, resulting in a higher chance of having an argument, resulting in a tense, toxic work relationship. At the same time, do not come off as aggressive and confrontational if something is taking place. If you do, it can result in you getting in trouble and coming off as combative or difficult. The moment you sense a conflict, act on it in a calm and professional manner.

The second step is to clarify what the issue is and what is causing the conflict to take place. Let's say two members of your team are arguing about how to move forward with a project. They are at the point where they can't come to the middle. The more they talk about it, the more they argue, resulting in work not getting done. Gather the facts of the situation before judging either teammate. Separate the teammates and ask them why they are acting the way they are regarding the situation. You are there to be neutral, act as a mediator with the goal of finding a solution that will work for both sides. Taking sides with one teammate can cause the other one to shut down. If they feel their professional opinion is not valued or they are not taken seriously, it can have a negative result on the production of the team.

The third step is to bring the teammates together, giving them a chance to explain their views on the situation. Encourage active listening, which is a way of listening and responding to another person that improves mutual understanding (United States Institute of Peace, n.d.). You want to encourage both teammates to explain their frustrations yet be able to work to come to a solution. The goal is for them to see what role each one played in the part and what they can do to come to a way to resolve the conflict.

The fourth step requires you to identify a solution. After both teammates have given their views of the situation, start to work on what can be done to resolve the issue. It can be something simple as sitting down and talking it out and putting some goals down to help take the next step forward. If both teammates are still unable to work something out, you are going to have to look at both sides and then come to a middle ground to create a solution. If you are in a situation like this, try your very best to be able to have a simple discussion and come to a solution. The last thing you want is to be locked in an argument and have to have someone higher up step in. In the long run, that can backfire. One, what you might want to do and what they decide is going to get done can be two very different things. Second, you do not want to come off as uncooperative, unprofessional, or unwilling to work with others who don't see eye to eye with you. At the moment, you might not think that it will have an impact. If it becomes a pattern, it can result in you missing out on opportunities for growth and development. You don't want to get stuck at a level because you were not willing to come to a middle ground.

The final step is to continue to monitor and follow up on the conflict. You want to make sure that communication improves between the two teammates, that the conflict is really resolved, and that everyone is on the same page. Don't assume that things are all peachy because you sat them down, and they said it was worked out. Actions speak louder than words. From a distance, keep an eye on things. If you see that the conflict really has not been resolved and tension is still there, work with the teammates to come to other alternatives that can result in a solution being found. The goal of this is to short-term resolve the dispute, but long-term you want to create a healthy, positive workforce environment in which everyone can be productive.

Setting goals is important for all of us, whether they are personal or professional. Make sure you are familiar with goal-setting tools that can help you establish what you are working towards. Make sure to follow the SMART goal guidelines, making sure your goal is specific, measurable, attainable, realistic, and timely. Consider the environment you are in when it comes to the workforce. Things such as emotional intelligence, conformity, and conflict resolution all have an impact on our work environment and our goals. Simple, short-term goals can lead us to complete the long-term goals we are aiming for. Take all these things into consideration as you move forward with your goals.

Things to remember:

Things don't always go as planned. To move forward and achieve your goals, be ready to make changes.

Strategically plan your personal and professional goals. Tools such as SMART goals, journaling, and vision boards are just a few tools you can use.

Do not ignore conflict. At one point or another, you will experience it. Understanding emotional intelligence, social conformity, and conflict resolution are important.

Resources:

Beresford, J. (2022). Thousands Sign Petition to Stop Dismantling of Iconic Bridge So Jeff Bezos' Yacht Can Pass. Newsweek. Retrieved from:

https://www.newsweek.com/thousands-sign-petition-stop-dismantling-netherlands-bridge-jeff-bezos-yacht

Bloomberg (2022). Bloomberg Billionaires Index, Jeff Bezos. Bloomberg. Retrieved from:

https://www.bloomberg.com/billionaires/profiles/jeffrey-p-bezos/

Brancaccio, D., Garretson, M., Conlon, R., and Shin, D. (2021). Is Amazon's high turnover a huge red flag or the secret to its dominance? Marketplace. Retrieved from: https://www.marketplace.org/2021/06/18/amazon-workforce-turnover-dominance-investigation/

Canva Pro (2022). My Vision Board. Created by Natalie L. Boehm on June 25, 2022.

Corporate Financial Institute (2022). SMART Goals. Corporate Financial Institute. Retrieved from:

https://corporatefinanceinstitute.com/resources/knowledge/other/smart-goal/

Ferreira, N.M. (2022). 400+ Motivational Quotes to Reach Your Potential Each Day. Oberlo. Retrieved from: https://www.oberlo.com/blog/motivational-quotes

Gassam Asare, J. (2022). Exploring the Ways Internalized Oppression Shows Up in the Workplace. Forbes. Retrieved from:
https://www.forbes.com/sites/janicegassam/2022/01/28/exploring-the-ways-internalized-oppression-shows-up-in-the-workplace/

Janin, A. (2021). How to Set Professional Goals and Plan Out Your Career. Wall Street Journal. Retrieved from: https://www.wsj.com/articles/how-to-set-career-goals-and-plan-out-your-professional-future-11605899711

Kashino, M.M. (2022). Three Things to Know About the Jeff Bezos Super Yacht. Washingtonian. Retrieved from: https://www.washingtonian.com/2022/02/04/three-things-to-know-about-the-jeff-bezos-super-yacht/

Kelly, J. (2021). A Hard-Hitting Investigative Report Into Amazon Shows That Workers' Needs Were Neglected In Favor Of Getting Goods Delivered Quickly. Forbes. Retrieved from: https://www.forbes.com/sites/jackkelly/2021/10/25/a-hard-hitting-investigative-report-into-amazon-shows-that-workers-needs-were-neglected-in-favor-of-getting-goods-delivered-quickly/

Krakoff, S. (n.d.). The Top 5 Conflict Resolution Strategies for the Workplace. Champlain College Online Blog. Retrieved from: https://online.champlain.edu/blog/top-conflict-resolution-strategies

Mental Health America, Inc. (2022). What is Emotional Intelligence and How Does it Apply to the Workplace? Mental Health America. Retrieved from:

https://mhanational.org/what-emotional-intelligence-and-how-does-it-apply-workplace

McLeod, S. (2016). What is Conformity? SimplyPsychology. Retrieved from:

https://www.simplypsychology.org/conformity.html

Shonk, K. (2022). What is Conflict Resolution and How Does it Work? Program on Negotiation, Harvard Law School. Retrieved from: https://www.pon.harvard.edu/daily/conflict-resolution/what-is-conflict-resolution-and-how-does-it-work/

United States Institute of Peace (n.d.). What is Active Listening? United States Institute of Peace. Retrieved from: https://www.usip.org/public-education-new/what-active-listening

Walt, V. (2022). Jeff Bezos gets a historic Dutch bridge dismantled so his $500 million yacht can pass. Fortune. Retrieved from: https://fortune.com/2022/02/03/jeff-bezos-historic-dutch-bridge-dismantled-koningshaven-rotterdam-500-million-superyacht/

Chapter 4

RESOURCES TO HELP YOUR CAREER GROW

"The only way to do great work is to love what you do. If you haven't found it yet, keep looking. Don't settle."- Steve Jobs

"It's not what you achieve, it's what you overcome. That's what defines your career."- Carlton Fisk

"Choose a job you love, and you will never have to work a day in your life."- Confucius

There are ways to educate yourself to grow your career without breaking the bank. In this chapter, I'm going to show you how you can gain knowledge and improve your goals even if you are on a budget. One thing is for certain, never stop educating yourself. The moment you do in any field, you are allowing others to get ahead of you. You want to stay focused on your goals, and part of that means having a willingness to learn.

I have found working in business, both for-profit and non-profit, how much we can learn from one another. Meeting other professionals is a must if you want to get ahead. I will be the first to admit this has been one of the most challenging things for me. As I stated in the previous chapter, my childhood was a very lonely one, not really socializing or learning the skills I needed to be around others. To be able to get past that, I have had to make the effort. Social anxiety is something that affects many people, and it is a very difficult thing to overcome. Even though I have improved, I know I have a long way to go. In the article, If Networking Makes You Anxious, Try This, the author sought advice from Dr. Susan Albers, a clinical psychologist from Cleveland Clinic. Here are the suggestions Dr. Albers suggests to help you decrease your anxiety and be able to approach people:

Visualize how things will unfold

Playing out in your mind how things will unfold can help you prepare for your event. What outfit are you planning on wearing that day? How will you start your day before attending your event? As you head to the event, envision what it will be like, not to overwhelm yourself, but to picture who will be there. Are there going to be people you know there? If so, take advantage of meeting with those you know to remain calm and uplifted. Then take the next step to introduce yourself to someone there you may not know. One thing you should try to avoid is thinking negatively, assuming that the worse situation will happen. It is easy to do so. Bring yourself back to the moment and focus on what is happening. Preparing yourself to be in the environment will benefit you

Write a script

Writing out a script ahead of time can help you in approaching people. This can be used in many ways, from how you introduce yourself to an elevator pitch. By doing this, you can help to alleviate any anxiety by preparing yourself. I have done this for elevator pitches in introducing myself and my organization. One thing I would suggest doing that was also suggested in the article is practicing in front of a mirror. The reason for this is you will be able to see your body language. If you are still anxious, you will see it in your body language and in your non-verbal behavior. This can give you a chance to see how you react and what you need to do to relax. If you are anxious when talking to others, they will very easily pick up on it. Allowing yourself to prepare can result in you being able to reduce your anxiety and having a more positive, energetic approach when meeting people.

Fuel up properly

The author pointed out in the article the importance of proper nutrition and nutrients that we need to be healthy. Dr. Albers pointed out that nutrients such as Vitamin D and magnesium are important for helping to buffer stress and relieve anxiety. Eating foods rich in magnesium is beneficial, especially days before your event can help in reducing stress. I take both Vitamin D and magnesium supplements because having epilepsy; I have anxiety and depression due to the side effects of my medication. I can say it has helped a lot. Another thing I use is a CBD patch which I have found very beneficial in alleviating stress and anxiety. Before attending the event, eat something so you will not be eating a lot while meeting with people; you want to focus on interacting and not appearing nervous or anxious.

Once you are at your event, the author put together some suggestions on how to adapt and take full advantage of being at the event:

Step outside of your role

Remember, when you take part in any event, people who don't know you see you as just another professional there. You are so much more than that. You are a human being. Being at events, you can talk about not just work but social things. Many that I have spoken to will talk about events in the community they attend or organizations they work with. One of the things the author suggested was being an advocate for those you help. In for-profit, it can be letting others know what your company is about and who you are helping. Being in a non-profit, I educate people I meet about epilepsy and why I am doing the work I am doing. Many people do not know what epilepsy is or that it even exists. Explaining my personal experiences and why I want better for the future of my community can show people that I am passionate about the mission of my organization and the seriousness of the programs we are creating. By doing this, not only can you connect to the person you are talking to, but they may also be able to connect you to someone who can help you.

Lower the stakes

Keep things simple when you are attending events. If, at this point, you don't feel ready to go around and give an elevator pitch, attend events where you can be there to listen and learn. Being an audience member and attending an educational event can help you to relax and be able to interact. Find events that have a discussion or panel that is in your field and use it as an opportunity to both learn and connect to others.

One thing that was discussed was the ten-minute rule. The author described that the point of the 10-minute rule was to give you a time or goal to engage with a person before moving on. There is more to the 10-minute rule than that. The 10-minute rule can also be applied to how long you can keep someone's attention. According to the article, *You Have 9 Minutes 59 Seconds to Hook Your Audience. Here's How to Do it in 3 Steps*; molecular biologist John Medina states you have 9 minutes and 59 seconds to keep your audience's attention. To get past ten minutes, you need to find active ways to keep your audience, or in this case, the person you are talking to, engaged. Take no more than ten minutes to introduce yourself, engage in a conversation, and at the end, hand them your business card. Let them know it was great to meet them, and here is how they can get in touch with you if they need anything. Make it a goal to get one of their cards as well. Keep any business cards you get from others and put them in a business card binder. You never know when you might need to collaborate with someone. After that, move on to the next person. Make it a goal for yourself to get at least a couple of business cards from others. As your confidence grows and you attend business events, continuing education seminars, depending on what your profession is, make it a goal to always leave, creating new connections. At first, it might not seem like much, but long term; you will see how many people you can truly connect with and the network system you will establish.

Once you find a balance and start feeling more confident about networking, that's when you want to kick it up a notch. Many professionals have challenges finding their own system in connecting to others. You must make that effort to do it if you want to grow and move forward. One resource I love is Forbes Magazine, to see how entrepreneurs have dealt with certain situations such as growth. In the article, 14 Steps to Take a Networking Pitch to the Next Level, each step was discussed by a different council member. All were excellent points, but the first one in the article really stood out. The step said to reframe networking as relationship-building. Some may ask, "Well, what is the difference?" When we first meet people, it takes some time before we can really connect with them and say that they are a friend. It is very much the same thing here. When you first meet someone, not knowing them can make you uncomfortable. I have found in attending events such as a Chamber of Commerce event there are some people with who you will connect and some with whom you just won't click. Don't go into these situations thinking everyone has to like you; everyone must connect to you. It won't happen, I can tell you that. I found when I was more active with my chamber, I connected to five members whom I felt were friends, and I could talk to them more about business and goals compared to others. A couple of people I met came off as toxic, and my goal was to give them their distance and focus on my own work. Follow your gut when it comes to meeting people. You want to make positive connections and be able to collaborate with others who will help you to move forward and reach your goals, not to fall back.

When it comes to continuing education, many do not continue to educate themselves, saying that the funds are not there to do so. If that is the case, there are many other resources to turn to in order to gain knowledge. There are low-cost or even free resources available that you can learn from. I can't tell you how much I have learned from reading books, Forbes, Harvard Business Review, and other creditable resources. I've gone online and done low-cost workshops to gain knowledge. My goal after finishing writing this book is to take a public speaking course to strengthen my skills. Right now, the course I want is out of my price range. Because of that, I am taking a course through Udemy, which was a little over one hundred dollars on public speaking given by Chris Anderson, who is head of TED. TED is known for hosting TEDx talks and inviting people to present numerous topics. Too many people use the excuse that because of money, they cannot educate themselves. My mother's mother immigrated from Belfast in 1948. She only went to school until she was fourteen and then went to work in the factory. Despite not going to school as long as many in America, she tested at a high school diploma level when she immigrated to the United States. Throughout her life, she read daily, trying to learn and gain as much knowledge as she could. She never went to college, but she was very good with numbers and money. She was in charge of all the finances in the house. So, at any point, if you start to think you cannot gain more knowledge, I want you to stop. You can learn something new every day if you put your mind to it.

To find the type of resources that are best for you, the first thing is to know what type of learner you are. Myself, I learn best when I watch something or experience doing it firsthand. When it comes to reading something, I must read it a few times before it clicks. Listening, I find I get bored easily and end up blocking so much of it out. There are quizzes online you can take to get a better understanding of what kind of learner you are.

There are four learning styles that people have. Many people do not have one set way of learning but learn from two or three styles. By understanding your learning styles, you are able to find the tools and resources you will need to accomplish your goal.

Visual learners are individuals who learn better through watching videos, drawing things out on a whiteboard, and observing a situation. Certain shapes, patterns, and other objects that can be observed can help visual learners retain material better. According to the article, 4 Types of Learning Styles: How to Accommodate a Diverse Group of Students, teachers who have students who are visual learners should make handouts for them and use presentations. I have watched videos on YouTube to learn, but make sure that they are creditable and not just something someone threw up there. An example of something I have used YouTube for is creating animation for videos to market my organization. One of my favorite visual resources is Khan Academy. It's free, and its founder Sal Khan has put a lot of great programs up there. Everything from courses for kids to things like economics. If you are preparing for a master's degree or applying to law school, you can study for your GMAT or LSAT for free. If you are a visual learner, resources like Khan Academy will be very beneficial to you.

Resources for visual learners are:

MindMesiter: a mind-mapping tool that helps visual learners be able to visualize what they are learning. It can create, share, and manage mind maps online and offline.

Bubbl.us: is another mind mapping tool that helps with charting out thoughts, stories, and homework. This is a free app for learners.

Visuwords: is an online graphically-based dictionary great for visual learners who want to look up the meanings of various words and concepts. It connects concepts and words to encourage retention.

TeacherTube: is similar to YouTube, except it is focused on instructional videos. It is a free site that has nearly every topic imaginable.

Pics4Learning: Free image library designed specifically for teachers and students. Has thousands of images on a variety of topics.

(Learning Path.org, 2008)

Auditory learners retain information that is reinforced by sound. Class lectures are a common way for students who are auditory learners to be able to retain information. For many, audiobooks are a great resource. A friend of mine is an auditory learner and will listen to audiobooks on his way to work and going home. I had a friend in college who would read her lecture notes out loud to herself to retain the material.

Resources for auditory learners are:

Audacity: is an easy-to-use audio editing software that lets you record and edit audio. It is free and works with many platforms.

NaturalReader: is designed to read text that is stored on your computer. You can have a free version or upgrade to have additional tools.

Free Audio Books: there are numerous sites that offer free audiobooks for people who enjoy listening to stories or learning information rather than reading about it.

(LearningPath.org, 2008)

Kinesthetic learners, also known as tactile learners, learn through experience. Many are "hands-on" learners. A friend of mine who is a mechanic is a kinesthetic learner. He has dyslexia and struggled in school with his classwork. However, he can fix any car you put in front of him. His wife manages his business, and he does the work. Kinesthetic learners are known for not being able to focus for very long. Once they can physically sense what they need to learn, they can comprehend the information better.

Resources for kinesthetic learners are:

Cram: allows people to create their own flashcards. There are many topics available.

Quizlet: is specifically designed to help students make flashcards and quizzes. They can also study from materials other students made.

Quia: gives both instructors and students resources. Instructors can create activities, quizzes, and surveys. Students can play activities and take quizzes.

(LearningPath.org, 2008)

Reading and Writing learners prefer to learn through written words. Based on the VARK Modalities Theory, these learners enjoy expressing themselves and learning through writing, journaling, researching, and reading (Malvik, 2020). According to the VARK website, a few examples of what reading and writing learners will use are lists, bullet points, and dictionaries. They will prioritize what needs to be presented and how to contribute it. When it comes to students learning, many will condense their notes, write things out again and again to retain the information, read and organize information to retain information. Professionals who are reading and writing learners enjoy using tools such as SWOT analysis, strategic planning, and carefully analyzing what others have presented.

Once you know what type of learner you are or if you are more than one, find out what style of learning is best for you. It can make it not only easier to learn but easier to do work by structuring things to the way you like it, that makes you comfortable. Don't worry about how others are doing things; focus on you. My husband is like a scanning machine, he reads it once, and it's there. It drives me nuts, honestly, how easy it is for him to learn. I have to watch videos, plan out what to focus on and re-read things before it finally clicks. That's why I must focus on my style and goals and not focus on others. It is easy to get lost or overwhelmed when you start focusing on others, so keep it simple: stay focused on you.

LinkedIn is a great resource not just for networking but for continuing to educate yourself. I have the basic premium plan, which is $39.99 a month or $239.88 a year if you pay the annual fee. There are courses to watch in leadership, management, marketing, professional development, and so much more. There are over 16,000 courses to choose from, so take advantage and watch and learn. If you cannot afford to take part in a certification program now, take part in some of the courses. You might find you can learn what you need from the videos, or you might study something such as lean six sigma and afterwards decide it would be in your best interest to take the course. That is what is great about LinkedIn learning. It gives you the chance to explore and see how far you want to go.

Social media marketing is something everyone should learn to do, even if you are not running a business. For those who feel anxious when networking, social networking is a great way to meet professionals and take the time to build a relationship with them. LinkedIn has been a great tool for many professionals to do just that. Many times, meeting someone virtually before meeting them in person can eliminate some of the anxiety in working with someone. In one of my favorite books, *Knock 'em Dead, Social Networking*, the author Martin Yate gives some great resources for social media and networking. Resources such as Google +, LinkedIn, Facebook, and Twitter are in there. The one social media site he really does not talk about is Instagram. You want to have an Instagram account for business. The reason is this; the younger generation prefers to use Instagram over Facebook. You can expand your target market, especially if you have a small business or organization. Having a business account, I am able to use tools for branding; you can create a shop, create ads, and watch videos to learn how to engage your audience and find more followers.

TikTok has become a resource for marketing, but I have mixed reviews on TikTok and do not use it to market my organization. Yes, you can create an audience, you can establish a brand, and promote it on TikTok. What I don't like about TikTok is some of the material you see really should not be there. For a short time, I did use TikTok to make mini commercials to get people to my YouTube channel to subscribe or to learn more about my organization. Every time I went on TikTok, though, some of the things I saw were just downright inappropriate. It made me not want to go on there, and I realized long-term it was not for me.

In the article, *7 Reasons TikTok Is Bad for Everyone*, the author lists seven reasons why not to have a TikTok account. I strongly agree with his article and suggest you vigorously research everything before using TikTok for any account, personal or professional.

ByteDance, the owner of TikTok, is a multinational company that operates in Beijing. Going to their website, ByteDance states under their Code of Conduct that they have high ethical standards and a culture of integrity. Actions from governments say otherwise. TikTok has been banned in India since 2020. Anyone in mainland China who uses China Mobile, China Telecom, or China Unicom is banned from using the app. Since 2020, the following countries have banned the use of TikTok:

India

Afghanistan

Pakistan (has banned it in the past numerous times, but then allowed access to it)

Bangladesh (was banned from 2018-2020)

Indonesia (banned for a week in 2018. Has allowed use again, but the government removes content in question)

The Indonesian government accused TikTok in 2018 of allowing access to pornography and other inappropriate forms of conduct.

(Maiorca, 2022)

Another reason people have been discouraged from using TikTok is it has led to decreased attention spans due to their videos being short. I can say many organizations like mine have seen the reaction to this. In having a YouTube channel, my videos are educational and can last anywhere from 5 to 13 minutes. I have tried to find ways to decrease the time and still give the educational information I need. I have made progress, but I find if the video does not get right to the point, the viewer is going to go away. According to the article, over sixty percent of users on TikTok are under 24 years of age. In the article, *Maturation of the adolescent brain*, the development and maturation of the prefrontal cortex occurs primarily during adolescence, and development is complete by the age of twenty-five. The development of the prefrontal cortex is very important for complex behavioral performance due to this being the region of the brain that accomplishes executive brain functions (Arain et al., 2013). When exposed to actions such as scrolling through one's smartphone, it has been shown to bring about sustained neurocognitive alterations due to changes in cortical regions associated with sensory and motor processing of the hand and thumb (Firth et al., 2019). The result can lead to changes in cognitive function, affecting our attention, cognitive function, memory processes, and social cognition.

Censorship is another major problem with TikTok. In fact, this is probably the main reason I do not like TikTok. Censorship has been used to limit underserved or marginalized communities from having a voice. In March 2020, *The Intercept* published the article *Invisible Censorship*, which stated that TikTok moderators were instructed to suppress posts from users that were "too ugly, poor, or disabled for the platform" (Biddle, Ribeiro, and Dias, 2020). The fact that my organization represents an underserved community with many being disabled, I don't care if the membership is free or not. I do not want any of my material on a site that instructs its moderators to act in such an unethical way.

TikTok is also known for allowing the posting of reckless dares or what they like to call "challenges." Challenges such as the Tide Pod challenge I still shake my head about. I thought when I was a teenager, we did stupid things, such as sneaking a couple of beers from my friend's father's fridge when watching a hockey game. I handed the tiara over to these guys after finding they were being dared to eat detergent pods, some actions resulting in death. The one that upset me the most was the "Seizure challenge," in which people were pretending to have seizures. I can tell you I have had so many seizures in my lifetime that I have lost count. I wouldn't wish a seizure on my worst enemy. Seeing that careless, reckless material is on TikTok makes me not want to use it as a resource.

TikTok is also known for collecting data on its users, so if you value your privacy, you're not going to get any using TikTok. TikTok can see what you are writing to your friends and others, making privacy non-existent. The Center for Internet Security warns users that TikTok collects data from its users that has sensitive information without their knowledge or consent. Collection of personally identifiable information, or PII, can be information such as age, image, personal contacts, relationship status, and preferences.

Security is a major concern with TikTok. Hackers have used SMS messages to get unauthorized access to people's accounts. One of the most concerning actions of TikTok when it comes to security and collecting data is it violates the Children's Online Privacy Protection Rule, which states that the PII of children under 13 cannot be collected (Center for Internet Security, 2022). Despite legal action being taken against ByteDance, TikTok continues to violate the rule.

The final concern the author had was the levels of harassment, abuse, and cyberbullying that take place on TikTok. Remember that over sixty percent of users are under twenty-four years of age. Many victims of cyberbullying are teenagers. According to the 2022 cyberbullying statistics, victims of cyberbullying are twice as likely to consider committing suicide, and many victims take part in self-harm behavior to deal with their trauma (Petrov, 2022).

What it comes down to is social media is going to be a tool you are going to have to use to market yourself professionally. You must be smart and do your homework to be successful, gain the audience you want, and prevent any complications. You want to steer away from companies that have been known to commit violations or continue to. LinkedIn offers many courses on social media marketing, strategy, and more. Udemy is also great if you feel you are not familiar with social media networks and need to find what works best for your goals.

There are times when educational resources only get us so far. There are times when professionals need help to get to the next level. I have worked with mentors and coaches as I have grown my organization and myself as a professional. When I first finished my MBA, I applied and was accepted into a program known as the Social Entrepreneurship, Engagement, and Development Lab, also known as SEED Lab, at U.C. Riverside. I won a full scholarship to take part in the program. It was intense, going weekly from September 2020 to May 2021. We had to come up with a project, create a business plan, find how we were going to fund our project, and how were we going to pitch to investors. It was a crazy number of months, but I can say it was the best thing I did because I learned so much. It also showed me that despite having an MBA, I was just starting to really learn what business was. Obtaining my MBA just laid the foundation for me to do so.

Hiring a career coach is a benefit for many. This is one area where you want to do your homework, and make sure that you find a coach that can help you with the goals you have. Coaches help people who are just entering the workforce environment, are starting or considering starting a business, or may be making a change in their career. Most coaches are focused on one area. In doing a search in my local area, I found there were over a hundred coaches in the area. Some were focused on career and strategic planning, some only worked with women, and others had a very vague description of what they did. The average cost was from $75 to $150 per hour. According to the article, Should You Hire a Career Coach?, $75-$150 per hour is the average. However, some who are in high demand can charge anywhere from $250 to $500 per hour (Renner, 2022). Research the person's background and any referrals or testimonials they may have. Remember you are investing in you, so make sure you have someone who is there to help you grow and focus on your goals. Examples of what career coaches do are helping to improve your resume, LinkedIn page, helping to network, researching ways to help one obtain a promotion or take their career to a whole new level.

The best time to hire a career coach is when you feel ready to make the next move in your career but don't know where to start. The best way to find a career coach is through referrals. Asking colleagues, friends, and other professionals if they know anyone is a great first step. Hearing firsthand from someone what their experience was can help you decide if this is a step you want to take. There are career coaches all over LinkedIn. Be careful when searching for a coach. When I first launched my foundation, you wouldn't believe how many people approached me, saying they were going to grow my organization to a whole new level if I hired them. The first thing I asked them was what was their experience in working with a non-profit? Many admitted to me that they worked mainly with clients who were focused on for-profit. Even though the goal is to make money in both, the approach you take and the way you plan it are different. The fact that they couldn't explain to me how to set goals for things like fundraising or collaboration made me skeptical. Because of this, I stayed in contact with classmates, communicated with my professors, and in time, started connecting to other professionals. The best thing to do when you start off is to learn from those around you in the field. Earlier this year, I read an article in the New York Post titled, *Is a career coach worth the money?* While the author said yes, it was worth it to invest in a career coach, I loved how he pointed out that if you don't have the funds, there are other means to gaining some insight. Gaining insight from your network is the first step, but if it is not enough, then invest in a career coach. It is excellent advice because you do not want to make any impulsive decisions. Set a budget, do your homework, talk to others, and when you decide that hiring a coach is the best option, then take that step.

As you grow and become more focused on what your long-term goals are, that is when investing in a mentor is important. Where a career coach can help you is with strengthening your resume, learning a new skill, or goal setting. Mentors work at a different level. Mentors work with people who have already strengthened their skills through a coach or their network and now want to focus on a leadership role. This is for professionals who may be in management and want to move higher up, someone who may already have a successful business and wants help strategically planning to take their company to the next level. Just like when you work with a coach, you want to have a mentor you can trust.

I have had two mentors in my lifetime. The first mentor I met while finishing my MBA. He was there to see what my goals were once I finished my degree. We grew up in a very similar culture, and we very quickly became great friends. Now he is on my board of directors and has been a great friend as we work to grow the foundation. Even now, when I feel overwhelmed, I have someone I can talk to if I feel my emotions are blocking any decisions I need to make. I can tell you as much as I love being an entrepreneur, and the excitement I feel when I achieve a set goal, it also has moments when anxiety and doubt can set in. It's at those points where you want someone you can trust and confide in to give their opinion from another point before you make any decisions. Sometimes we can be our own worst enemy, and having people around us who can help us move past that is essential.

My second and current mentor has been helping me with a few goals. The first has been supporting me as I write my book, the second is growing my foundation, and the third has been what I want to do in the for-profit world. The thing that I have found to be beneficial is that along with my mentor educating me on how to take the next step, he also listens to the experiences I have had personally and professionally, and we learn from one another. Communication is essential if you are going to work with a mentor. In the article, *The Importance of Mentors and Sponsors in Career Development*, the author describes mentorship as a two-way street, meaning as they help to educate you, they are learning from working with you. What has helped us to grow and work together is we both have experienced some very difficult life experiences and understand that what we went through, as hard as it was, we are still here for a reason. The goal is to make the very best of that.

The one thing I had to learn, working with my mentor, is how to take a different approach to failure. My passion when I was younger was to be an attorney. I wanted to be independent, with no husband, no kids, no commitment, nothing. I just wanted to live my life the way I wanted, to travel, be with friends, and just give one hundred percent to everything I did. Having multiple seizures in my last year of undergrad, losing my license, and just doing everything to have the energy I needed to finish my classes was the first sign I wasn't going to law school. At that time, I didn't see this as a bump in the road; I saw it as a failure. For years, I tore myself apart, feeling what I had set out to do was never going to happen. I even questioned why I went to college in the first place. I felt because I did not achieve my goal, I shouldn't have gone down the path of trying. Now today, of course, I know that it's not true. Obtaining a higher education was the best thing I have done for myself and even my children.

In my experience, working with different mentors has given me the idea of the kind of person I want to work with. There have been a couple that I have been very happy with and some that I could not connect with at all. If you are working with someone and it's not working, move on. Don't hesitate to do so. Once you feel you know a mentor's style and it is just not working, there is nothing wrong with moving on. It's the same when I was talking about coaching. The majority of coaches and mentors are great, but it comes down to personalities and work styles. As great as someone may be, they may not click with you. Make sure if you are going to invest in a career coach or mentor, you feel comfortable working with them, and they are there to help you reach your goals.

Sponsorships are another great way to advance your career and take things to the next level. Unlike a mentor, sponsors are internal colleagues at a higher level who can support and promote you (JP Morgan Chase & Co., 2021). They will work and use their influence to advocate for you and help you get promoted and move to the next level.

In the article, *The Importance of Mentors and Sponsors in Career Development*, there are three steps you must follow to have a sponsorship opportunity. Now, doing these steps does not guarantee anything, but it puts you in a positive spotlight and increases the chances of getting noticed.

The first step is making sure that you are contributing to the organization and that others see your efforts. Make sure the work you are doing is credited to you and not others. There are people who are more than happy to take credit for the hard work others do and have no problem getting promoted to a position that they didn't really earn. Don't be just physically there but be known to others. Be a team player that helps to create a positive climate and help those who need help. By demonstrating leadership skills, good communication skills, and that you have a positive outlook and attitude, the chances that you will get noticed will increase.

The second step is being willing to come out of your shell, step out of your comfort zone, and be willing to be challenged. Fear of change is what holds most people back in their careers. Be willing to work with others and learn from them. As you work on projects with your team, make it clear that you want to learn, you want to grow, and you want to get ahead. When you are willing to take on new tasks, learn new material, and grow, it demonstrates leadership. Do not be afraid of change or challenges. It is how you grow and how you develop into the person you want to be, both personally and professionally.

The third step is networking. As we talked about earlier in the chapter, this can be the most challenging step. Overcoming social anxiety about how to approach other professionals can be a learning experience. Being a team player can help you to establish relationships at work that may not have happened. Attitude is a little thing that makes a big difference. You want to find a balance when working toward being a leader. If someone needs help, guide them, and help them to learn so they feel valued. If you come off as bossy or feel you are above others, that is a red flag for other leaders. The last thing they want is for someone who is negative to be leading. Negative leadership leads to a toxic environment. The result is employees who have potential leave for other positions, high turnover, situations arising where human resources must get involved, and if bad enough, you get terminated.

Another amazing experience that only a few get to experience is a fellowship. Normally when you think of a fellowship, you think of graduate school. For example, someone working toward a Ph.D. or specializing in a certain area of medicine. Now there are career fellowships that you can take part in to learn new skills and grow. On the website ProFellow, there are paid fellowships to help you advance to the next level. Examples of paid fellowships are in journalism, economics, innovation, global business, and more. The competition is very high as ProFellow lists on their home page that there are 2,294 fellowships listed, with 205,241 applicants applying.

There are Federal Government Fellowships as well. On the U.S. Department of State website, there are five professional fellowships available. Many of these require higher education, such as having a Ph.D. with a science background or engineering. One was for mid and senior-level professionals in the for-profit and non-profit sectors, and one was Veteran-focused. These fellowships are not for entry-level positions. The federal government is looking for individuals in leadership positions who are not only willing to grow but are willing to advise. Many of these positions ask for people to either be at an expert level or a high level of consulting. If you have the experience or at least meet the basic requirements, do not be afraid to apply. The worst situation is that they say no.

There are many resources available to help your career grow. At the end of the day, it will be your actions that will decide how far you move up. You have the capability to do so with the right tools and guidance. Come out of your shell, be confident, let others know you are ready for the challenge and be ready to give one hundred percent. That will lay the foundation for opportunities to open for you.

Things to remember:

Education is important for growth. Along with using resources, find out what kind of a learner you are to be able to use the right tools.

Working with a career coach can help you to grow and achieve goals. Mentors can help you work towards leadership positions.

Sponsorships can help you get promoted in your current career. Having a sponsor can help you network with others and bring you to a higher level

Resources:

Arain, M., Haque, M., Johal, L., Mathur, P., Nel, W., Rais, A., Sandhu, R., & Sharma, S. (2013). Maturation of the adolescent brain. Neuropsychiatric disease and treatment, 9, 449-461. https://doi.org/10.2147.NDT.S39776

Biddle, S., Ribeiro, P.V., and Dias, T. (2020). Invisible Censorship. The Intercept. Retrieved from: https://theintercept.com/2020/03/16/tiktok-app-moderators-users-discrimination/

ByteDance (2022). Our Mission Inspire Creativity, Enrich Life Code of Conduct. ByteDance. Retrieved from: https://www.bytedance.com/en/

Center for Internet Security (2022). Why TikTok is the Latest Security Threat. Center for Internet Security. Retrieved from: https://www.cisecurity.org/insights/blog/why-tiktok-is-the-latest-security-threat

Coombs, A. and Arcand, J. (2022). 21 Inspirational Career Quotes. Work it Daily. Retrieved from:

https://www.workitdaily.com/inspirational-career-quotes/3-work-to-become-not-to-acquire-elbert-hubbard

DePaul, K. (2022). If Networking Makes You Anxious, Try This. Harvard Business Review. Retrieved from: https://hbr.org/2022/05/if-networking-makes-you-anxious-try-this

Firth, J., Torous, J., Stubbs, B., Firth, J.A., Steiner, G.Z., Smith, L., Alvarez-Jimenez, M., Gleeson, J., Vancampfort, D.,

Armitage, C.J., & Sarris, J. (2019). The "online brain": how the Internet may be changing our cognition. World psychiatry: official journal of the World Psychiatric Association (WPA), 18(2), 119-129. https://doi.org/10.1002/wps.20617

Forbes Coaches Council (2022). 14 Steps to Take a Networking Pitch to The Next Level. Forbes. Retrieved from: https://www.forbes.com/sites/forbescoachescouncil/2022/07/01/14-steps-to-take-a-networking-pitch-to-the-next-level/?sh=5b006c231fd7

Gallo, C. (2018). You Have 9 Minutes and 59 Seconds to Hook Your Audience. Here's How to Do it In 3 Steps. Inc. Retrieved from: https://www.inc.com/carmine-gallo/you-have-9-minutes-59-seconds-to-hook-your-audience-heres-how-to-do-it-in-3-steps.html

Giangrande, G. (2022). Is a career coach worth the money? New York Post. Retrieved from:

https://nypost.com/2022/03/13/is-a-career-coach-worth-the-money/

GoldenRule (n.d.). 10 Inspirational Career Quotes- Start your success story today. GoldenRule. Retrieved from: https://www.goldenrule.co.za/10-inspirational-career-quotes-start-your-success-story-today/

JP Morgan Chase &Co. (2021). The Importance of Mentors and Sponsors in Career Development. JP Morgan Chase &Co. Retrieved from:

https://www.jpmorganchase.com/news-stories/the-importance-of-mentors-and-sponsors-in-career-development

LearningPath.org (2008). 30 of the Best Educational Tools for Auditory, Visual, and Kinesthetic Learners. LearningPath.org. Retrieved from:

https://learningpath.org/articles/30_of_the_Best_Educati onal_Tools_for_Auditory_Visual_and_Kinesthetic_Learners.h tml

Maiorca, D. (2022). In What Countries Is TikTok Banned? Make Use Of. Retrieved from:

https://www.makeuseof.com/what-countries-is-tiktok-banned/

Malvik, C. (2020). 4 Types of Learning Styles: How to Accommodate a Diverse Group of Students. Rasmussen University. Retrieved from:

https://www.rasmussen.edu/degrees/education/blog/typ es-of-learning-styles/

Petrov, C. (2022). 50 Alarming Cyberbullying Statistics to Know in 2022. Tech Jury. Retrieved from:

https://techjury.net/blog/cyberbullying-statistics/#gref

Price, D. (2021). 7 Reasons TikTok Is Bad for Everyone. Make Use Of. Retrieved from:

https://www.makeuseof.com/is-tiktok-bad/#:~:text=Many%20security%20researchers%20have%20fo und,and%20HTTPS%20when%20delivering%20videos.

ProFellow (2022). 20 Paid Fellowships for Your Mid-Career Sabbatical. ProFellow. Retrieved from: https://www.profellow.com/fellowships/paid-fellowships-mid-career-sabbatical/

Renner, R. (2022). Should You Hire a Career Coach? Business News Daily. Retrieved from:

https://www.businessnewsdaily.com/10919-hire-career-coach.html

U.S. Department of State (2022). Professional Fellowships. U.S. Department of State. Retrieved from:

https://careers.state.gov/interns-fellows/professional-fellowships/

Vark (2022). Read/Write Strategies. VARK Learn Limited. Retrieved from: https://vark-learn.com/strategies/readwrite-strategies/

Chapter 5

FORMS OF COMMUNICATION

"The art of communication is the language of leadership." – James Humes

"The less people know, the more they yell." – Seth Godin

"Talent wins games, but teamwork and intelligence win championships." – Michael Jordan

Communication is challenging for so many professionals in multiple fields. I have seen miscommunication in the medical field, in legal, in business, you name it. The challenge is that many people have no training in communication and, even with the highest education, lack the skills to communicate properly. To establish yourself as a leader, learning to communicate with your colleagues is going to be essential. Having great communication skills can lead to opportunities that can help grow an individual and help to grow the organization of which they are a part.

Communication is defined as a process by which information is exchanged between individuals through a common system of symbols, signs, or behavior. Communication can also be a verbal or written message. There are multiple ways we communicate as humans. All of us have worked with people who are straightforward and honest, as well as people who are passive-aggressive. Personalities can clash, resulting in frustrations which can lead to miscommunication and unnecessary gossip. If there is any advice I can give you from both a personal and professional perspective, stay away from gossip. You do not want to engage with people who enjoy stirring the pot and causing unnecessary trouble, especially if it is intentional.

To be able to improve communication skills, we need to define the different communication skills and how to use them properly. As you learn about communication skills, make it a goal to improve your communication skills. We all have some level of weakness, yet we can learn from it and become stronger.

Verbal communication is defined as the use of words or language to convey a message. Conversations, speeches, presentations, or a simple phone call all fall under verbal communication. Verbal communication is important in leadership because it is considered an important tool to get the information needed to teams to help companies function at the level they need to. There are many things that make up verbal communication, not just saying words. The tone of voice, the words that are used, the speed at which one talks, how words are pronounced all come together to create verbal communication.

There are four types of verbal communication, intrapersonal, interpersonal, small group, and public.

Intrapersonal communication is when the sender and receiver of the information are the same person. Think of saying something out loud to yourself when you are thinking or trying to figure something out. I have found this one of my best tools for problem-solving when working at my computer.

When my husband and I shared an office, it drove him nuts, and he would tell me that I was talking to myself again. I would jokingly tell him that as long as I don't answer myself, then I'm still doing okay.

Interpersonal communication is between two individuals, just between the two of them. Examples can be a casual conversation over coffee or talking on the phone with a friend or colleague. Interpersonal communication is the first level in which non-verbal communication has an influence on how the other person may perceive what the person is telling them. For example, if you tell someone to have a nice day, but your non-verbal behavior shows you are frustrated with them, it sends mixed messages. That's why it is important to have an understanding about different levels of communication. You want to make sure that the message you are trying to get across comes out the way you want it.

Small group communication is just that, communication between a small group of people. Examples of small group communication can be a meeting, a small business team having lunch together, where more than two people are present, but it is not considered a large group.

Public communication is when a large group of individuals gather to hear information from others. Examples of this can include a continuing education conference, seminars, press conferences, political campaigns, and public speaking events.

Nonverbal communication is defined as the transfer of information through body language, facial expressions, and gestures. Nonverbal communication is important because people are watching and observing many things as you speak. Whether you are having a casual conversation or are in an important meeting, you want to be aware of the message you are sending.

In the article, *9 Types of Nonverbal Communication and How To Understand Them*, the author lists nine types of nonverbal communication and what message that nonverbal communication may be sending.

The first is body language. If someone is happy and engaged, they will greet you with a smile, their cheeks raised and looking energetic. Now, if someone is tense and folds their arms when talking to you, that sends a message of anger or anxiety. Anger and anxiety are a turn-off for many in any environment, both personal and professional. Anger and anxiety are emotions we all have at some time; the importance is how to handle them. If you show anger and anxiety in the workforce on a regular basis, it sends a message to your team that you really do not want to be there; you do not want to be engaged. That hurts your team and you as well. It can lead to lost opportunities and even chase away employees that have potential and can bring opportunities to the company.

Movement is the second nonverbal communication behavior. Sitting at a table, talking in a meeting, having dinner with a client, in any environment like this, your movement is being watched. To make a positive impression, sit up and become engaged. Even if it is a meeting where you would very much like to be somewhere else, stay engaged. It will be remembered by your colleagues, supervisors, clients, and anyone you meet with. If you are fidgeting, looking at your watch, looking around the room, all those actions say you are not focused and in the moment. To many, it says you are not interested in what is taking place. For people who want to move up in leadership, this is the last thing you want anyone to see. Many leaders, in fact, find it quite disrespectful when an employee is not focused and shows behavior that they do not want to be there. I can say it is a pet peeve of mine, especially if I am working with students and interns, trying to mentor them and help them set goals. I can very quickly figure out who is interested in learning and who is just there to get some volunteer hours they are required to have. To the ones who are interested, I will go up and beyond to help them reach their goals. For those who I can tell are just going through the motions, I do the opposite.

Posture is the third nonverbal communication. Posture, the way someone holds their body when they are standing, or sitting, can send many messages. Sitting up straight, shoulders back, and making eye contact with a person demonstrates that one is engaged in the conversation. Someone who is slouched down and looking at the ground demonstrates that the person may be bored, tired, and does not want to be present or engaged.

Gestures are the fourth nonverbal communication. A gesture is defined as a movement, usually of the body or limbs, that expresses or emphasizes an idea, sentiment, or attitude (Merriam-Webster, 2022). Examples of gestures are finger-pointing, moving of hands while talking, waving of arms, and running one's fingers through their hair. In the article, *Gesture's role in speaking, learning, and creating language*, the author points out that even congenitally blind individuals who have never seen someone gesture move their hands when they talk, demonstrating the role that gestures play in communication.

Space or the distance we have between someone we are talking to, is the fifth form of nonverbal communication. When first meeting someone, you may stay a couple of feet away from them, establishing boundaries. As humans, we can be territorial because it gives us a sense of control. Once people get to know one another, they feel more comfortable, for the most part standing side by side. Space can also show a sign of status, or social rank, such as a leadership position. The supervisor of the department may get the corner office while others are working in cubicles.

Paralanguage is the sixth form of nonverbal communication. Paralanguage is unique, however, because it involves both verbal and nonverbal communication that influences meaning, tone, intensity, pausing, and even silence (the University of Minnesota, n.d.). The American Psychological Association defines paralanguage as the vocal but nonverbal elements of communication by speech. An example would be if I read something off a piece of paper sarcastically, but when you read what was on the paper, you wouldn't think of any reason for it to be said that way. My tone was negative, but there was nothing negative written on the paper. These are known as paralinguistic cues or paralinguistic features (APA,2022).

Facial expressions are the seventh form of nonverbal communication. Facial expressions can include eyebrow movements, raising or lowering of the face, and tensing of the jaw or mouth. Facial expressions I have found to be one of the easiest ways to see how someone is truly feeling, no matter what they are saying. Many people cannot hide what they are thinking, and the best way to get an idea of what they are thinking or how they feel is by following their facial expressions.

Eye contact is the eighth form of communication. For some people, it is very challenging for them to make eye contact. It may be due to trauma, having a neurodivergent condition, or being shy; there are a number of reasons. The challenge for this is many find not making eye contact a form of being disrespectful and can be a turn-off. In business, it is very important that you be able to make eye contact, especially if you are in or entering a leadership position. Tools people can use to improve making eye contact can be practicing in a mirror or talking to those they feel comfortable around. If making eye contact is a challenge for you, set goals to improve your ability to make eye contact and carry out a conversation.

Touch is the ninth form of nonverbal communication. A common form of touching when first meeting someone is a handshake. Other forms of touching, such as putting your hand on someone's shoulder or hugging, should only be used once you get to know the person and their boundaries. What might be a good intention to you might make the next person very uncomfortable.

Written communication is communication through any written document. Examples of written communication are emails, texts, letters, reports, or memos. All forms of communication are important, but to me, written communication is one of the most important ones. Written communication can work for you or against you depending on the situation. Once you send an email or a text, it's there forever. If you wrote something out of anger and let your emotions get the best of you, it can be held against you. If someone denies saying they are going to do something, but you have a text stating they would, you just proved they were being dishonest.

Written communication skills are essential no matter if it is for personal or professional use. Applying for an apartment, a job, to go to university, you need to have good writing skills. According to the article, *A Complete Guide to Effective Written Communication*, your written communication should be comprehensive, accurate, appropriate, have good composition, and be clear. If you are writing a letter trying to get into a program, you want your letter to get right to the point about why you should be accepted. Focus on keeping things simple, use an active voice, and stay on topic. If you ramble on, you will lose the interest of the person reading it. It is best to have someone read it over before submitting it. When I have had to write important letters, apply for different programs, or help put programs together, I always have someone review it. Recently, I started helping a few organizations here in my area create a workforce development program. After doing the draft, I sent it to three professionals who are part of the project for their professional opinions. I asked not just for positive feedback but also for constructive criticism. The reason for this is that there may be a mistake we do not see, or rewording things in a different way may make our presentation or argument stronger. A second set of eyes is always beneficial.

Visual communication is the practice of graphically representing information to efficiently and effectively create meaning (ITM, 2021). Examples of visual communication are graphs, infographics, animation, data visualization, iconography, and illustration. Visual communication is important because many people learn more easily than through written or verbal communication. When I created the educational information for my nonprofit, I decided to offer it in both written and visual forms. For those who retain information easier by reading, they can go to our blog and read articles. For those who learn better visually, they can go to our YouTube channel and watch the videos. Both have the same information; it is just presented in different ways.

The advantage of visual communication is that it can be delivered in a more direct way, can easily get someone's attention, and establish credibility. Putting visual information together is very time-consuming, and often, other forms of communication are needed, such as written and verbal communication. When I make the videos for our educational channel, I create them from articles my research interns or I have written. Then I have to find the right pictures for the slides and write up things the way I want them to be. Depending on the topic and how much information there is, one presentation may take an hour, and some of them, though, a few hours. I enjoy making visual presentations to get the message across, despite the extra time they take. I find visual presentations are a great way to teach others and get important information to your audience.

Feedback communication is the practice of one person letting another person know how they can improve their communication skills. Think of a leader or mentor advising one of their teammates or students how to improve themselves as a professional. This is one of the trickier forms of communication because either someone takes on the challenge of improving themselves or takes it personally and shuts down.

If there is anything I can advise you to take into consideration is who is giving you feedback and how they approach you on it. I have been very lucky that I currently have a mentor who is straightforward and is honest with me about my journey as a professional. I have gained strength in many areas, and there are other areas on which I need to focus. I am very organized and a good goal-setter. I have accomplished a lot of short-term goals that I felt I would not have at this point. My weakness is, I feel I need to get so much done or I have not been productive. At one point, I was working seven days a week, averaging fifty to seventy hours a week. It caught up with me, and my mentor told me if I wanted my health to improve and be a productive entrepreneur, I had to stop what I was doing, that it was destructive at many levels. He told me I was to stop working on Sundays and have a day with my family, do something nice for myself, anything but getting in front of my computer and working. Sounds easy to the average person to be told to take a day off, but it was a challenge for me. I finally followed my mentor's advice and started taking off Sundays. The first couple of times, I felt guilty, feeling I was allowing myself to fall behind. Then it started to be enjoyable, having more time with my sons, going for hikes again, working in my garden, things that brought me happiness. I started getting more energy, and my anxiety went down. Years back, I wouldn't have taken his advice; I would have kept up my destructive behavior. I realized I needed to make a change, and that is why I have my mentor — to point out the positive things I am doing and to help me with my weaknesses.

As leaders, it is important to give your team members constructive criticism and help them set goals to become more productive. At the same time, do not forget to compliment them on the great things they are doing. You want to keep things in balance and help your team to feel they are being productive and that they have a great leader that will support them.

Make an effort to let your team know that they are doing great on a regular basis rather than just an annual review. If someone does a great job on a project or gets a contract with a company you have wanted to collaborate with, let them know they did a great job. Just saying something brief like, "I saw you got the deal for us; great job keep it up," can improve your team member's self-esteem and make them feel like they are part of the team. Little things like that are positive and, in time, add up in a good way. You will have a team that wants to be there, that wants to be productive and lead the way.

When you are communicating with a team member, make sure it is at the right time and in the right environment. If someone has a disagreement with someone, don't confront them there. It will cause more anger and resentment. If you confront someone about their work using constructive criticism in front of their colleagues, it will embarrass them. They will feel called out and that their work is not appreciated. That, in time, can lead to high turnover rates and losing valuable team members.

If you have to give feedback to a team member, meeting with them, just the two of you, can be more productive than in a group setting. Being in a group setting can cause unnecessary anxiety and drive team members to shut down. Sitting down and helping them set goals can be more productive. Give examples of what you want your team member to work on and help them to see their challenges from a positive view. Instead of telling someone that they have shown they can't do something, say instead to them, "I see you have been having challenges with this task, but I think by making some changes, you will be able to accomplish your goal."

The most important thing is to follow up with your teammates. The biggest mistake I have seen leaders make is meeting with their team members once a year, going over everything, and then not talking to them again until the next year. Be willing to meet more than once a year, let them know if they are having challenges, to schedule an appointment with you. You need to keep communication lines open if you are going to create a strong team and have a healthy climate where people are being productive and successful. If you are not a leader but working toward being one, the examples I have shown here are what you should be expecting from your supervisor. If you find that it is not happening, or the leaders of your organization are not willing to take those steps, it is best to start looking for a company that has the same values that you have.

Mass communication is the act of a person, group of people, or organization relaying a message through a channel of communication to a larger group of people or organizations (Denomme and Grimsley, 2021). There are many forms of mass media that can get information out to a specific group of people or can be used to get information out at a global level for a large audience.

Print media is one form of mass communication. Examples of mass communication are magazines, newspapers, books, novels, journals, and publications. Print media has become more digital over the years, with many reading their favorite newspaper or magazine online or on an app. Despite the changes due to technology, print media still remains important, with many choosing to still buy their favorite magazine at the airport to read or enjoy an afternoon at the public library.

Broadcast media focuses on radio, television, recorded music, and movies. The entertainment industry has created a multimillion-dollar industry through broadcast media producing films of many different genres, and entertaining people throughout the world. According to the article, *Types of Mass Communication*, more than ninety percent of people consider film and television as their sources of entertainment. Music records, considered the first form of non-print mass communication, have evolved over time, providing different types of music we love. We went from records, eight-track tapes, and cassettes to compact disks. Today, with just the touch of your finger, you can download your favorite songs to your cell phone or tablet, enjoying listening to your favorite songs commercial-free.

Outdoor media is used to market services to an audience. Billboards will have advertisements depending on where you are going, showing restaurants, shows, products, and services. Driving on the freeway, my least favorite ads to see are the billboards from attorneys telling you to call them if you have been in an accident. Once in a while, when I have traveled to Vegas, I love seeing what comedy shows are available at the hotels on the strip. There is a need for all of those advertisements because there is always going to be someone who either wants or needs the service.

Transit media is similar to outdoor media, but instead of the billboards you see on the freeway, these are the posters you see at the bus stop, the metro rail, or subway. They play the same role as outdoor media, trying to get you to buy something or use a service. Taking the train to work, you may see an advertisement from Mcdonald's for a cup of coffee and an Egg McMuffin. It looks great in the picture, and then you remind yourself in reality what it is really going to taste like. The point is to get your attention and hope you are hungry enough to stop in and get breakfast.

Digital media has transformed media, becoming one of the most cost-effective forms of media. Digital media has opened the doors for people to advertise through mass email, podcasts, blogs, websites, and social media channels. Digital media has been the way I have been able to reach my audience for my nonprofit. Using tools such as Instagram, Facebook, Twitter, YouTube, and LinkedIn, I have been able to connect to people on a global level and create revenue doing it. Amazon has made money by offering e-books on its site, getting people to read and share their thoughts. Digital media continues to grow and create opportunities for those who benefit from it.

All of these forms of mass communication are beneficial for those seeking a larger audience. Digital has been the leading form of mass communication for so many in recent years, especially during times such as the Covid pandemic. Many companies and organizations feared they were going to go under, and being able to mass communicate and meet with clients virtually gave them a chance to network and stay operational. Each form of mass communication has its own needs and can benefit many professions across the field.

In reviewing the different ways, we communicate as humans; you can clearly see how important communication is on a personal or professional level. In fact, communication is important in life, no matter what the situation is. My closest friends and colleagues are the ones who are upfront with me, are honest, and are ready to tell me what they truly feel. Because I know what they are saying to me, and they mean it, I can fully respect them for it, even if it is something I don't agree with. I can respect how they feel and agree to disagree with them. There are many benefits to being a good communicator when it comes to life in general. Here are some of them:

Building trust and relationships

Creating new opportunities

Personality

Resolving Conflicts

Expressing ideas and personal needs

Standing out from others

Decision Making

(Barot, 2021)

Establishing trust benefits us in numerous ways. Word gets around, and trust is something you want to be known for. It helps not only to build relationships, but it also helps because people will be willing to help you network, knowing you are an honest person. It will help to create opportunities for you, both personally and professionally. Many of the projects or events I have been invited to take part in have been because of establishing creditability for being honest and serious about my work.

Personality plays an important role in communication. The more we are engaged with people, the more we have to learn to adapt to others. Having a good personality, establishing yourself, and demonstrating good character are all important. You want to present yourself as a professional and be positive, even when someone who is toxic comes around. You want to be the team player who can get past the toxicity and, if possible, avoid it at all costs.

Do not be afraid to express yourself when it comes to your work and your well-being. It is important to find a balance between the two to prevent burnout and be productive. Finding a balance can help you to stand out and establish yourself as a leader. Decision-making is important because many are fearful of making a decision. Too many people in leadership cannot make a decision. They will find every reason not to give an answer or make it look as if it is something they are reviewing, and then they never get back to you. Their goal is they are hoping you will forget about it, and by doing that, the problem that needs to be addressed gets ignored. This is what leads to dysfunction in an organization.

There is always room for improvement in communication. One thing you want to avoid is bringing toxicity into your work environment. At the beginning of the chapter, I pointed out that you should, at all costs, avoid gossip. When someone is labeled a gossiper, it is a negative label to have. Gossip is the spreading of rumors, reports, or subject matter. The bad thing about gossip is that the more the story goes around, the more it gets changed. It is one thing to have a conversation about a colleague. Gossip, however, is often about the misfortune someone is having, such as going through a divorce or they were denied a promotion. If it is a subject that you would not repeat to the person being talked about, right there, that tells you it is gossip and to stay out of the conversation.

If a work environment is taken over by gossip, it can cause damage to the work climate. Trust levels go down, performance starts to decline, polarization takes place as people choose sides, and eventually, people leave due to the toxicity it is causing. The worst thing is that many who will walk off are the ones who were there to be productive and establish a career. Don't allow gossipers to destroy the climate and chase good, hard-working employees away, having a negative impact on the entire team.

So, what can one do to get rid of gossip in the workplace? In the article, *9 Ways to Get Rid of Workplace Gossip Immediately,* the author gives nine steps to get rid of workplace gossip.

Enact a 'zero-tolerance policy

This is one of the best things companies can do to protect employees. Make it clear from day one that gossip will not be tolerated. If someone breaks the rule, set consequences depending on the severity of the gossip. It can be anywhere from a write-up to termination, depending on what was said and the impact it had on the employee being gossiped about.

Set an example

Setting a positive example and not engaging with gossipers is good because you will be able to establish trust with others. This can be very challenging because it is very easy to get into a click with people, and when they don't show the best of character, breaking away can cause unnecessary stress, and even you become part of their gossip. From experience, I can tell you if they are gossiping about other employees, they are most likely gossiping about you as well. It's best to steer clear of that drama.

Let the boss know

This is easier said than done because it can go either way. If you have a good boss, he will put an end to it quickly, not wanting the climate in their department to become toxic. If you have someone who does not care, sadly, things will not change. Follow your gut and do what you feel is right.

Address the perpetrators

Sometimes the best thing you can do is call someone out for their unprofessional behavior. Be careful how you go about it. I had a bad habit in the past of being blunt and to the point. Do not do that; take a neutral approach with them so they don't become defensive. Be professional in explaining why talking about others is not the right thing to do. If they become defensive, ask them if they would like it if someone were talking negatively about them.

If you're a manager, meet with your team

This is the best thing you can do as someone in a leadership position. Make it clear that behavior like this is not acceptable and that there are negative consequences to gossip.

Encourage positive gossip

Personally, I don't like the term positive gossip. If anything, I would say encourage positive stories and positive feedback. You want to enforce a positive climate to work in. Talk about positive things in the workforce, such as a team member's accomplishments with a project or someone who went above and beyond for a customer. If it is a personal story, make it something positive such as a vacation someone went on or a good restaurant you went to and wanted to recommend. Remember to reinforce the positive climate.

Ignore the gossiper

If everything else has failed, ignore them. If telling the boss or confronting them has not worked, the best thing anyone can do is to stay away from them. If you can't stay away from them, when they come by and start gossiping, turn back to your work and ignore them. If they say anything, simply say, "I have to finish what I'm working on. I don't have time to talk right now." Put an end to the situation right then and there.

Turn it back on the gossiper with a positive thing to say

When someone starts gossiping and saying something negative about a team member or situation, respond with a positive comment. It will prevent them from going further into negative gossip. After a few times of doing that, most likely, the person will not come by to gossip anymore.

Keep your private life private

I can't stress how important this last one is. Unless you can absolutely trust someone, it is best not to talk to anyone about your personal life. If you are facing a crisis situation such as domestic violence, mental health problems, or marriage problems, do not talk about it in the office. Go to your human resources department and see if your company has an employee assistance program (EAP). Many companies can help you if things are not going well. Many employee assistance programs will offer you a number of free sessions to talk to someone while you find a provider through your insurance. If you are trying to get away from an abuser, many can help you find organizations that will help you relocate. If your employer does not provide those services in many areas, you can call 211, and they will help you. Speaking about private, sensitive subjects just fuels gossip and can make your situation worse.

To improve your communication skills, there are many routes that you can take to gain knowledge and experience. There are numerous videos on YouTube to watch. Be careful what you choose and make sure it is a creditable source. My suggestion is to subscribe to the Harvard Business Review channel. It is free, and on their playlist, *'The Harvard Business*

Review Guide', you will find a lot of videos here focused on communication. Everything from '*The Art of Active Listening,*' "*Working with a Passive-Aggressive Coworker,*" "*Controlling Your Emotions in an Argument,*" and many more topics that fall under communications.

LinkedIn Learning has many free resources to watch to improve your communication skills. There were four hundred twenty-eight courses available when I searched communication. Courses on interpersonal communication, working with difficult people, effective listening, and speaking up at work were just a few of the many. You will not get as much information here as you will taking a certification, but if you are looking for a few pointers, *LinkedIn Learning* is a great resource.

Coursera is an excellent resource for finding low-cost or free certifications. In just searching "communication skills," I found seven hundred and nine courses available. Many of the certifications that were available were from the University of Michigan, the University of Pennsylvania, Yale, and other creditable academic institutions. To take the course and not get the certificate was free; if you wanted the certificate, it was as low as forty-nine dollars. Take full advantage of low-cost or free resources and make the effort to educate yourself. Simple things add up and can put you well ahead of the game compared to those who make little to no effort.

If you want to take a certification from an academic institution that will provide excellent information, I have taken classes at the University of California at Los Angeles in their extension program. The few classes I have taken were very well put together, and the professors who taught them picked very good literature to learn from. Just like anything, you get what you pay for. For the Business Communications Certificate, the estimated program tuition was five thousand two hundred and fifty dollars, with a two-hundred-dollar application and candidacy fee and an estimated cost of eight hundred dollars for materials and textbooks. I suggest a course like this if you are working towards a leadership position, need to improve your communication skills, or your employer gives you a certain amount of funding yearly for continuing education. This is not just for learning a few pointers or if you are curious. This is to expand opportunities in your career, move up in your company, or make a career change.

When it comes to books, I recommend reading *TED Talks: The Official TED Guide to Public Speaking*. Even if you do not plan on going into public speaking, this book provides a great deal of knowledge in knowing how to communicate with groups. If you're not going to get in front of an audience but in front of a team to present a project, you can use the same techniques. You may be giving facts about a project rather than telling a story, but you are using the same structure. Knowing how to get in front of others and communicate is essential for those who want to work up to a leadership position.

Magazines such as the *Harvard Business Review*, *Forbes*, and the *Economist* have many articles focused on communication. If you are not ready to subscribe or are not sure if you want to, all three magazines allow you up to three articles a month free. I subscribe to *Harvard Business Review* and *Forbes*. I love reading the *Economist* and feel they provide great information, yet I feel the regular subscription fee is overpriced. For a digital subscription to *Forbes*, I pay forty-nine dollars a year, and for *Harvard Business Review,* it's one hundred twenty dollars a year for a digital subscription. An annual digital subscription for the *Economist* is one hundred and ninety-nine dollars. If you are a student or an educator, there are discounts. For college students, the annual digital fee is forty-nine dollars and seventy-five cents a year. It is the same for educators. For any magazines, newspapers, or sources you like to read and learn from, always check to see if they have a student, educator, or any type of discount. When I was working on my MBA, I had a student discount for *The Wall Street Journal* at four dollars and ninety-nine cents a month and the same thing with *The New York Times.* Subscriptions can add up fast, but having access to resources like this can be a great way to learn.

There are multiple ways to communicate, and as humans, we each have our own strengths and weaknesses when it comes to communication. Never think of a weakness as something holding you back, but something you can work on, improve, and turn into a strength. Focus on improving your communication skills in the workforce and even in your own personal life. Take full advantage of the resources you can find and set goals of becoming better at communication. For those who are leaders, remember to communicate with your team on a regular basis and not just at their annual review. Establish a professional relationship and help your team members set goals, grow, and become better, more productive team members. Establish respect and trust to help them achieve what they need to, establishing a positive climate in their work environment. Establish rules to prevent toxic behaviors such as gossip and focus on creating a healthy, positive environment for everyone to work in.

Things to remember:

1.	There are many forms of communication, both verbal and nonverbal. It is important to understand the different forms of communication and how they can affect how your message is received.

2.	It is important to give feedback as a leader to your team. Along with compliments, giving constructive criticism is important. Focus on helping your team set goals and feel valued.

3.	Keep toxicity out of the working environment by enacting a 'zero tolerance' policy to prevent gossip and if negative gossip is taking place, encourage your team to come to you to resolve the situation.

Resources:

American Psychological Association (2022). APA Dictionary of Psychology: Paralanguage. American Psychological Association. Retrieved from:

https://dictionary.apa.org/paralanguage

Barot, H. (2021). 13 Reasons Why Communication Is Important In Life. Frantically Speaking. Retrieved from: https://franticallyspeaking.com/13-reasons-why-communication-is-important-in-life/

Business Terms (2018). Verbal Communication: Definition and Types. BusinessTerms.org. Retrieved from: https://businessterms.org/verbal-communication/

Denomme, D. and Grimsley, S. (2021). Mass Communication Overview & Examples. Study.com. Retrieved from: https://study.com/learn/lesson/mass-communication-overview-examples.html

Dunne, C. (2019). 40 Team Communication Quotes to Inspire Your Team. Tameday. Retrieved from: https://www.tameday.com/team-communication-quotes/

Goldin-Meadow, S., & Alibali, M.W. (2013). Gesture's role in speaking, learning, and creating language. Annual review of psychology, 64,257-283.

https://doi.org/10.1146/annurev-psych-113011-143802

Indeed Editorial Team (2022). A Complete Guide to Effective Written Communication. Indeed. Retrieved from:

https://www.indeed.com/career-advice/career-development/written-communication

ITM Institute of Design and Media (2021). Why is Visual Communication an Important Skill to Learn. ITM Group of Institutions. Retrieved from: https://www.itm.edu/blog/idm-why-is-visual-communication-an-important-skill-to-learn

Keiling, H. (2022). 9 Types of Nonverbal Communication and How to Understand Them. Indeed. Retrieved from: https://www.indeed.com/career-advice/career-development/nonverbal-communication-skills

Leadership Now (2022). Leading Thoughts: Quotes about Communication. Leadership Now. Retrieved from:

https://www.leadershipnow.com/communicationquotes.html

MasterClass (2022). Feedback on Communication: 8 Tips for Effective Feedback. MasterClass. Retrieved from: https://www.masterclass.com/articles/feedback-on-communication

Merriam-Webster. (n.d.). Communication. In Merriam-Webster.com dictionary. Retrieved August 27, 2022, from https://www.merriam-webster.com/dictionary/communication

Merriam-Webster. (n.d.). Gesture. In Merriam-Webster.com dictionary. Retrieved September 4, 2022, from https://www.merriam-webster.com/dictionary/gesture

Merriam-Webster. (n.d.). Gossip. In Merriam-Webster.com dictionary. Retrieved September 13, 2022, from: https://www.merriam-webster.com/dictionary/gossip

Presentation Point (2019). How can Visual Communication be Applied to Enhance Communication? Presentation Point. Retrieved from:

https://www.presentationpoint.com/blog/visual-communication-to-enhance-communication/

Purbey, P. (2022). Types of Mass Communication. Getmyuni. Retrieved from:

https://www.getmyuni.com/articles/types-of-mass-communication

Schwantes, M. (n.d.).

University of California at Los Angeles (2021). Business Communications Certificate. UCLA Extension. Retrieved from:

https://www.uclaextension.edu/business-management/leadership-management/certificate/business-communications

University of Minnesota (n.d.) Types of Nonverbal Communication. University of Minnesota Libraries. Retrieved from:

https://open.lib.umn.edu/businesscommunication/chapter/11-2-types-of-nonverbal-communication/

Chapter 6

FACING CHALLENGES

"Obstacles are those frightful things you see when you take your eyes off your goal." - Henry Ford

"Being challenged in life is inevitable, being defeated is optional." - Roger Crawford

"Only those who dare to fail greatly can ever achieve greatly." - Robert F. Kennedy

Working on improving oneself to advance in a career, education or bettering oneself is easier said than done. Many of us have challenges due to past experiences. The purpose of this next chapter is to focus on overcoming any negative experiences that could hold you back from being the person you truly are. The attitude I want you to come in with is that this is all about you, and as you read this, make goals on how you can be happy, healthy and live life the way you want it to be.

As we face our personal and professional goals as humans, a lot of times, the one thing we need to work on to succeed is ourselves. Many people, however, put the needs and wants of others before their own well-being. 'Selfless' is defined as having no concern for oneself, acting in an unselfish way (Merriam-Webster, n.d.). Being an individual who is selfless takes a lot of strength due to the responsibilities they take on. The opposite is being selfish, which is defined as being concerned excessively or exclusively with oneself, seeking or concentrating on one's own advantage, pleasure, or well-being without regard for others (Merriam-Webster, n.d.).

How do we find a balance between the two? No one likes being around people who are selfish and can't see past themselves. At the same time, as much as we want to help others, if we don't help ourselves, we can feel the effects of it long-term in a negative way. Studies on such topics led to the creation of positive psychology. Positive psychology is a branch of psychology that is focused on the character strengths and behaviors that allow individuals to build a life of meaning and purpose — to move beyond surviving to flourishing. (Psychology Today, 2022).

Positive psychology was founded in 1998 by former APA President Martin E.P. Seligman, Ph.D. and Claremont Graduate University psychology professor Mihaly Csikszentmihalyi, Ph.D. (Azar, 2011). Rather than focus on conditions that caused negativity in someone's life, such as depression, Dr. Seligman and Dr. Csikszentmihalyi focused their studies on what makes us thrive as humans and promoting mental health. According to the article, *Positive Psychology and Physical Health,* the topics of concern in regard to positive psychology are:

Positive subjective experiences (happiness, gratification, fulfillment, flow)

Positive individual traits (strengths of character, talents, interests, values)

Positive interpersonal relationships (friendship, marriage, colleagueship)

Positive institutions (families, schools, businesses, communities)

Experiencing happiness, having a positive character, having great friends, a strong marriage, and being affiliated with great organizations and communities are very important for all of us. Positive psychology is interesting because when we first think of psychology, we think of what is wrong; we think of conditions such as anxiety, depression, bipolar disorder, and things that are associated with negativity and stigma. Mental health should not be focused on just the negativity we face as humans. To be able to thrive, we need to focus on our strengths, not just weaknesses.

What areas can we focus on that will lift us up and bring us happiness rather than feeling anxious or depressed? Two things that many struggle with are self-esteem and self-confidence. Self-esteem is having confidence and satisfaction in oneself (Merriam-Webster, n.d.). Psychology Professor Carol K. Sigelman refers to self-esteem as "your overall evaluation of your worth as a person, high or low, based on all the positive and negative self-perceptions that make up your self-concept" (Bailey, 2003). We all have positive and negative views of ourselves. The importance is finding a balance between the two and how to approach each one. In the article, *The Foundation of Self-Esteem*, the author breaks down what we focus on about ourselves:

Who one is (one's philosophy of life and character)

What one does (one's tangible and/or intangible work products regarding people, nature, objects, or oneself)

What one has (one's inherent, developed, or acquired qualities and quantities)

The different levels in how one appears (one's physical body, personality, and reputation)

To whom or what one is attached (God, a concept of a "special" person or group, money, possessions, or power).

(Bailey, 2003)

Self-confidence is defined as having confidence in oneself and in one's powers and abilities (Merriam-Webster, n.d.). Where self-esteem is focused on having confidence in yourself as a person, self-confidence is now applying what abilities and talents you have to it. Self-esteem and self-confidence overlap and have an effect on each other. If you are happy with who you are, you are then confident in what you need to do to accomplish things and have a happy life. If you are not happy with who you are, then you will lack the confidence or hesitate to do things that you most likely can accomplish but doubt that you can.

If you find that you are someone who lacks self-esteem or self-confidence, there is no shame in that. Many people do, and I'll be the first to tell you I am still working to improve my own self-esteem and self-confidence. I'm better than where I was years ago, but I still get social anxiety, feel I'm being judged when a lot of the time I'm really not, and at times beat myself up when it comes to body image or how I feel I must come off to others. What is important is that you don't allow it to become so bad that it is debilitating — resulting in it having a negative impact on your relationships, your career, and any goals you have set for yourself.

First and most important is taking the time to practice self-acceptance. We are who we are for a reason. One thing I tell my mentees when I am working with them is to focus on finding what their talents and passions are. When they do and apply that to the goals they set, the results can be very rewarding. As they go through and work on their goals, mistakes will be made. Those mistakes do not make them a failure. When we make a mistake, the goal is not to repeat the mistake but to learn from it.

There can be many challenges in why someone has a hard time practicing self-acceptance. I have found through talking to many people who are successful the hardest thing was having to accept who they were. For example, my best friend is gay, and I have other friends who are part of the LGBTQ+ community. Many have told me that they know who they are and were not ashamed to be that way. Where their fear lay was what their family or friends were going to think. It is a very legitimate fear, and it's sad that in this time and age, we still see a great deal of discrimination against people in the LGBTQ+ community. The fear of the unknown of what others may think can have a huge negative impact on one's self-esteem and self-confidence. Deciding to be open about having epilepsy was a challenge for me. I knew that the moment I decided to tell others about my experiences of having a neurological disorder, many opportunities that I may have if no one knew would be taken off of the table once I did say something. I made up my mind, though, that in order for me to help others, I had to accept that having a neurological disorder was part of my journey in life and that I had to face it. Facing any challenge when it comes to self-acceptance is easier said than done.

Many people who lack self-esteem and self-confidence tend to look at things from a negative perspective. Start trying to take a more positive approach to something. Find ways to surround yourself with more positive people and find others who can relate to you. Many organizations have support groups, and since Covid, have kept a lot of their zoom groups active. I have joined a few support groups since, and it has had a positive impact on my mental health. Being able to meet with others, even if it is just once a week, is a great way to talk about things others may not be able to relate to. It is a great way to create friendships, even if you are meeting more virtually than in-person. When it comes to facing challenges, healing and becoming stronger, I meant every word at the beginning of this chapter when I said it is all about you. To achieve overall wellness, you have to invest in you. Only then can you help and make a difference for others.

Wellness is a holistic integration of physical, mental, and spiritual well-being, fueling the body, engaging the mind, and nurturing the spirit (Stoewen, 2017). Many times when we think of our health, we think about our physical health, how we look, diet and nutrition, what people see on the outside. That is only a fraction of what it takes to achieve wellness.

According to the article, *Dimensions of wellness: Change your habits, change your life*, there are eight interdependent dimensions: physical, intellectual, emotional, social, spiritual, vocational, financial, and environmental. While all are important for us, the author states that they do not have to be equally balanced. This makes sense seeing how if we tried to balance them out all equally, we would be heading towards perfectionism, which is the last thing we want to aim for. The goal is to find how each of these applies to your life and at what levels you feel balanced.

Dimensions of wellness

Physical Dimension

Caring for your body to stay healthy now and in the future

Intellectual Dimension

Growing intellectually, maintaining curiosity about all there is to learn, valuing lifelong learning, and responding positively to intellectual challenges

Expanding knowledge and skills while discovering the potential for sharing your gifts with others

Emotional Dimension

Understanding and respecting your feelings, values, and attitudes

Appreciating the feelings of others

Managing your emotions in a constructive way

Feeling positive and enthusiastic about your life

Social Dimension

Maintaining healthy relationships, enjoying being with others, developing friendships and intimate relations, caring about others, and letting others care about you

Contributing to your community

Giving your talents and time to help others in your community

Spiritual Dimension

Finding purpose, value, and meaning in your life with or without organized religion

Participating in activities that are consistent with your beliefs and values

Vocational Dimension

Preparing for and participating in work that provides personal satisfaction and life enrichment that is consistent with your values, goals, and lifestyle

Contributing your unique gifts, skills, and talents to work that is personally meaningful and rewarding

Financial Dimension

Managing your resources to live within your means, making informed financial decisions and investments, setting realistic goals, and preparing for short-term and long-term needs or emergencies

Being aware that everyone's financial values, needs, and circumstances are unique

Environmental Dimension

Understanding how your social, natural, and built environments affect your health and well-being

Being aware of the unstable state of the earth and the effects of your daily habits on the physical environment

Demonstrating commitment to a healthy planet

Resource: Dimensions of wellness: Change your habits, change your life (Stoewen, 2017)

Reviewing these dimensions, you can easily break them down and create goals for yourself to improve your overall well-being. You may find that in some dimensions, you have strengths and others weaknesses. To start, pick three dimensions that you feel you need to improve on. Create a goal for each of the three you picked. Make it into a SMART goal as we worked on in the previous chapters.

Example: Goals to improve overall wellness

1st Dimension: Emotional

Focus: Managing emotions in a constructive way

Goal: to reduce anxiety

Specific: want to reduce anxiety levels and improve mental health

Measurable: keeping a journal to see what can be triggering anxiety

Attainable: Finding resources to reduce anxiety (meditation, yoga, breathing techniques) and using them

Realistic: establishing an environment to carry out and work on goal (use resources)

Timely: six months

Smart Goal:

In six months, I will establish healthy habits to reduce my anxiety and improve my mental health. I will practice breathing exercises daily and will do yoga and meditation at least three times per week. I will document when I have episodes of anxiety with the goal of finding my triggers and working on ways to prevent them.

Pick any three you would like and set them up the same way as the example above. Make sure to set a reasonable goal, and if you have to, make changes do it. Exercises like this can make you feel overwhelmed at times, but the goal is to gain strength from them and see what you truly need to improve on. It can be something simple that takes a couple of weeks or something more challenging, like the example I created above, for which I set a goal of six months. Start simple and then start to make more challenging goals for yourself. If something starts to be just too much, you can leave it and make a goal to go back to it. There have been goals I have wanted to accomplish that I realized I was not ready for. If that happens, set a specific date on which you will try again and review your goal.

Working towards overall wellness is easier said than done. In order to find wellness, many of us have to heal from past negative experiences. Trauma is one thing that prevents many from achieving wellness. The word trauma is the Greek word for "wound," which was used to explain physical injuries (Merriam-Webster, n.d.). Today the word trauma is used to explain not just physical but emotional injuries as well. There are many situations that can create trauma in someone's life. Survivors of domestic violence, serving in combat, child abuse, a serious injury, all of these can result in someone being traumatized. The thing that our healthcare system in America has failed to do is help with not just physical healing, but emotional and mental healing as well.

Trauma has many effects on the body, but what many fail to understand is the impact it has on the human brain. There are three parts of the brain that deal with stress; the amygdala, hippocampus, and prefrontal cortex. The amygdala, which is part of the limbic system, is primarily involved in processing emotions and memories that are associated with fear (Guy-Evans, 2021). The amygdala is responsible for regulating emotions. However, when someone has been traumatized, they can become aggressive very easily. Many would feel the person is overreacting to a situation. This situation is known as amygdala hijacking or losing control of one's emotions. The term was created by Daniel Goldman, author of the book *Emotional Intelligence: Why It Can Matter More Than IQ* (Guy-Evans, 2021). The goal of the term was to recognize that the amygdala is designed to respond swiftly to a threat, even if it is real or not (Guy-Evans, 2021).

The challenge that many who have experienced trauma face is the fact that it cannot tell the difference between physical and emotional threats. The result is that someone reacted in an aggressive way when the reaction was not necessary. Many people who are in this situation have been diagnosed with Post-Traumatic Stress Disorder (PTSD). The American Psychiatric Association defines PTSD as a psychiatric disorder that may occur in people who have experienced or witnessed a traumatic event such as a natural disaster, a serious accident, a terrorist act, war/combat, or rape or who have been threatened with death, sexual violence, or serious injury.

Along with the amygdala being affected by trauma, the hippocampus and pre-frontal cortex are affected as well. According to the article, Traumatic stress: effects on the brain, studies have shown evidence of smaller hippocampal and anterior cingulate volumes as well as decreased medial prefrontal and anterior cingulate function. What happens here is when someone is triggered, and the amygdala reacts, the pre-frontal cortex and hippocampus do not have the time needed to signal to the limbic system that things are okay. The result is the overreaction and rage behavior many with PTSD show.

If you are experiencing symptoms of anxiety, depression, or PTSD, I can truly empathize with you because it is something I have dealt with for many years. Anxiety and depression due to the side effects of my anti-convulsant medication and PTSD due to childhood trauma and medical trauma. When I told a friend of mine who has epilepsy herself, that if I had to choose between epilepsy and PTSD, I would rather deal with epilepsy, she became so upset with me. I told her that medication controlled my seizures and that if I was having a bad day, I knew what to do; I had the tools needed to keep things under control. At that point, I had not figured out what I needed to do to keep my triggers under control when it came to PTSD. What many fail to understand is that with epilepsy, a lot of people have auras or warnings that they are going to have a seizure or know what will trigger one. I have found that even though I know what triggers my PTSD, the simplest things can trigger it. My medical trauma is due to a nurse sexually assaulting me. For years something as simple as a nurse taking my vitals sent my anxiety levels through the roof. The nurse was not hurting me or being disrespectful, but just the fact that the nurse was so close to me or touching me that I had to close my eyes and count while they did their job. I look back at that time and think, why did I get so upset over nothing? Then I remind myself what happened and that I have moved on from it.

When I started to see a therapist for my PTSD, the therapist had me keep a journal to see what I was experiencing in my daily routine and if there were any situations that would cause me to be triggered. The best thing my therapist did for me was let me know as I started to talk about my traumas things were going to come up from my subconscious, things I wouldn't want to experience again. I would feel worse before better. I am grateful she warned me because if she hadn't, most likely, I would have stopped therapy the moment it started. Once I got past that point, it was the first step in getting past being angry and allowing myself to have some peace in my life.

If you have experienced trauma, it is so important to get it under control and heal. Long-term trauma can cause so many long-term chronic illnesses, affecting one's health. Chronic stress from trauma increases cortisol levels, which is a stress hormone. It can cause hormonal imbalance, resulting in weight gain, even if you eat well and exercise. Trying to get your hormones under control when living with chronic stress can be very challenging. The best thing you can do for yourself is to seek help. The challenge we have here in our society is the stigma that has been placed on mental health. I personally feel that seeing a therapist is something all of us should have access to. Even if it is something like going in and venting about any frustrations with work, family, or something personal, it is essential. Being able to establish a healthy client-therapist relationship has been a key factor in being able to move forward and work toward success. Many cannot afford it due to insurance not covering it, or worse; they are afraid or worried about what others will think.

Many people, when they have experienced trauma, feel negative feelings such as guilt or shame. Shame is something that no one should have to face when they are a survivor of a traumatic event. In the article, *Ashamed and Afraid: A Scoping Review of the Role of Shame in Post-Traumatic Stress Disorder (PTSD)*, the authors describe shame as a painful set of affective and cognitive states typified by self-judgment stemming from a perceived transgression of social/cultural norms or expectations. The two negative emotions, guilt and shame, play a role in the trauma, but each has its own unique role. Guilt is a negative evaluation of a specific behavior, feeling that one has done something horrible, whereas shame is used to condemn oneself, labeling themselves as an awful person (Saraiya and Lopez-Castro, 2016). I can say I felt guilt and shame when it came to my medical trauma. I did not tell anyone when it happened, and seven years after it took place, I relived it through a nightmare. I felt guilt in having to tell Tobias what happened, and I felt shame that when it took place, I froze and did not fight back. The result was dealing with a lot of anger, and even though I didn't want anyone to know I was feeling it, you could clearly see through my body language something was wrong. The one thing that helped me heal was therapy and obtaining my MBA. Getting rid of the anger and working towards being a better person really laid the foundation for me to move past this as a stronger person.

Trauma affects us all in different ways, but at the end of the day, everyone deserves to have a happy life and achieve wellness. Do not be afraid to seek help and use the tools you need to help heal. If you are going to succeed both personally and professionally, your overall well-being must be a priority to do just that. Don't worry about what others think; take care of yourself so that others can see your potential and what you truly are capable of.

There are other things that can hold someone back or create doubt that they can move to the next level or even feel they deserve to. Imposter syndrome, also known as perceived fraudulence, refers to an internal experience of self-doubt and believing you are not as competent as others perceive you to be (Frothingham, 2021). Some of the most successful individuals battle imposter syndrome. Many feel what they have accomplished or achievements they have made they don't deserve. According to the article, *You're Not a Fraud. Here's How to Recognize and Overcome Imposter Syndrome* – **there are five main types of imposter syndrome:**

Natural Genius

People who are natural geniuses can learn things with little to no effort. When they feel they cannot accomplish something, they are afraid of failure. Tobias is a natural genius, and I'll be the first to admit I wish I had the level of intelligence he has. Tobias is able to read something once or look at a map once, and then it's in his brain for good. When he immigrated to the United States from Germany, he was told it would take him five years to complete his bachelor's degree due to needing to improve his English. He finished his degree in three years with honors and was teaching many native Hawaiians how to speak and write English. His organic chemistry teacher once told me, "There was Tobias, and then there was the rest of the class." Two of his chemistry professors kept in touch with him for many years, proud of what he had accomplished. When going on to get his dental degree, he got a perfect score on his DAT and then graduated number two in his class out of fifty dental students. The University of Buffalo offered him a position to do research and earn his Ph.D. Anything Tobias decides to do, he can do it and then some.

Where I have found Tobias to show symptoms of imposter syndrome at times is if he is not challenged, he feels he is failing. Working at the university clinic, a lot of the procedures he has done for years, he is now becoming bored with. There are new treatments due to advancements in technology, but because of a limited budget, the university cannot supply him with the tools he needs to do them. When Covid took place, it really bothered him not being able to be in the clinic to help patients. After restrictions were lifted, going to work has not been the same for him. He decided to obtain an MBA, and his goal is to open a dental institute. He feels due to the lack of resources; what his patients need, he can't give them. It frustrates and upsets Tobias that he cannot do more or worse; he has to refer them out to private practice. Many of the patients cannot afford private practice costs, which means, most likely, they won't go and seek treatment. It is then he feels he has failed to help the patients who are coming into the clinic. Even though he knows what he needs to help them, the university cannot supply him. He takes pride in his work, and when he cannot do something, he pins it on himself.

The Perfectionist

Individuals who are perfectionists have a hard time setting realistic goals and feel anything they do, the results have to be the highest they can be. They are afraid to fail, and even when they do accomplish something, they will find something wrong with it. A friend of mine who has epilepsy is a journalist. I have seen over the years how hard she is on herself. She is always striving to have everything perfect because she feels she has to prove despite having epilepsy, she can do her job. I can tell you she is very smart and gifted, and it shows in her work. Many people have discriminated against her on the job, and when someone does, she has to give one hundred percent and then some to show them she is capable of doing her job. I have seen her get sick plenty of times due to the stress this has caused her. Even though many of us in the community have told her how proud we are of her, I feel at times that she questions if we really mean it.

The Soloist (Rugged Individualist)

The soloist is someone who prefers to work alone and feels that they will not achieve success unless they work on it themselves. In many situations, they will reject help, feeling they must accomplish their goals on their own. If they have to accept help, they feel they have failed themselves by not being able to complete their goals on their own. Many people in this situation experience burnout due to taking on so much.

The Superhero

People who fall under the superhero feel they have to be the best at everything they do. Even though I don't think of myself as a superhero, I have pushed myself to be the best at what I need to do. When it comes to being in a leadership position, I need to set a positive example for those who work with me. I need to present to my board the results they want to see. When it comes to my children and their care, I will advocate making sure they get the very best care, no matter the impact it has on me. When I was in graduate school, even though my children were four and six at the time, I felt I had to accomplish as much as possible to set a positive example for them. The result was that when I felt I was not giving one hundred percent; I was failing at my goals. Even if I did well in a class, if there was something I felt I could have done better, I was ready to tear myself apart. The result was that I became depressed and exhausted, which led to me getting sick. It took a long time before I could convince myself that I couldn't always give one hundred percent, and I had to learn to find a better balance with what I needed to do.

The Expert

People who fall under this are focused on a topic that they are passionate about. For many, this can fall into their profession. They work to learn as much as they can and, despite their intelligence, feel they still don't know enough. Many feel if they don't know what they need to know, they will underrate themselves, feeling inadequate. They cannot find satisfaction when it comes to their work or their accomplishments.

Imposter syndrome has a negative impact, resulting in a number of situations. Many fear asking for a promotion, feeling despite their accomplishments, they don't deserve the promotion. Many experience burnout when they feel they are not contributing enough and, in time, feel they cannot fulfill the requirements of their position, despite their accomplishments. When it comes to accepting responsibilities, many will ask for smaller ones, feeling if they take on a challenging task, they will automatically fail at it. Self-doubt can play a role in imposter syndrome, with many feeling they cannot accomplish their goal, despite having the ability to do so. When they do accomplish their goal, many contribute it to luck or someone or something that made it possible. When setting goals, many will set very high goals that can be challenging to accomplish, resulting in them being upset when they cannot complete the goal in the time they feel they should. Imposter syndrome also has a negative effect on one's mental well-being. Anxiety, depression, lack of self-confidence, and shame are just a few examples of the negative feelings one with imposter syndrome faces.

One thing that many people fear feeling is vulnerability. Vulnerable is defined as one being capable of being physically or emotionally wounded, being open to attack or damage (Merriam-Webster, n.d.). Vulnerability is often considered a weakness. Often people think if you are vulnerable, that you can easily be used, taken advantage of, or naïve of what is going on around you. Vulnerability can, however, be a tool for us to gain strength and grow.

Brené Brown, who is a researcher focused on studying vulnerability, describes vulnerability in a very different way. Brown states, "vulnerability is the core, the heart, the center of meaningful human experience" (University of Minnesota, 2016). What can cause a feeling of uncertainty and risk can be turned into a feeling of joy.

When I first launched my nonprofit organization, I had an experience in which I felt vulnerable. One of my board members, who was a volunteer for SCORE at the time, suggested I meet with a mentor to make sure I understood what I needed to do for the foundation. I reached out to SCORE, and they put me with someone who didn't have nonprofit experience. From the beginning, I could tell she was not happy to be assigned to me. When discussing what my goals were for the foundation and the void I was trying to fill, she did everything to try to discourage me. One day she clearly stated to me, "There's no reason for you to even exist." I had enough of her and made an excuse to end the meeting. I had to walk away from my desk, I was too upset even to work. I went into my kitchen and looked out the window, and started to think, "Was she right about this? Was there a reason for me to launch this organization?" At that moment, I felt vulnerable, second-guessing myself and wondering if I was capable of accomplishing my goals. It was at that point I reminded myself why I decided to launch my foundation. I was filling a void for my community. The larger organizations were focused on research, lobbying, and 'finding a cure' or 'creating awareness.' I knew they were not creating awareness because so many people I have met do not understand what epilepsy is or that it even exists. Neurologists, neurosurgeons, neuroscientists, lobbyists, pharmaceutical companies, biotech companies, and universities were the ones they were networking with in order to gain funding. When it came to what it was like to live with epilepsy, discrimination in the workforce or in healthcare, and the negative effect epilepsy has on someone's mental health; I knew the larger organizations were clueless because many working there are working for a paycheck to push their mission, not to improve the quality of life for those dealing with epilepsy. I knew after living with epilepsy for forty years at that point it was now or never if I was going to launch this organization. I knew there was a chance that people might not take my work seriously or with the complications I have had with my health, something might happen, and I would not be able to fulfill my duties. To deal with the vulnerability I was facing, I did two things. First, I stopped working with the SCORE mentor. I didn't need her toxicity around me. Second, I created an exit strategy just in case something did happen. I told myself if a worse situation arose, I could create a blog and YouTube channel to educate others and manage those if the foundation did not grow. I am grateful that I did not allow feeling vulnerable to stop me from achieving what I wanted to.

Despite the challenges I have faced at times with my health and building an organization, it has been one of the most rewarding experiences and has pushed me to continue to educate myself and grow as a professional.

I encourage you to read this chapter more than once and go through it to see if there is anything you are truly facing. If you have experienced trauma or are having challenges with your mental health, please take care of yourself and research the resources that are available to you. I also encourage you to research even more than I have provided here. I have found the greatest thing that helped me heal was doing research, learning about what was affecting me, and setting goals to deal with my challenges in a healthy way. Remember, there is no shame in seeking help, and at the end of the day, you matter.

Things to remember:

Positive psychology focuses on character strength. It is important to find a balance between being selfless and selfish. It is important to have empathy for others, but we also need to have empathy for ourselves and our well-being.

We all need to focus on our overall wellness to find happiness. The dimensions of wellness are all important, and we should all set goals to achieve wellness.

It is necessary to heal from trauma to gain wellness. Fear and shame are two feelings that are common for individuals battling PTSD. Do not be afraid to seek help if you need it.

Resources:

American Psychiatric Association (2022). What is Posttraumatic Stress Disorder (PTSD)? American Psychiatric Association. Retrieved from:

https://www.psychiatry.org/patients-families/ptsd/what-is-ptsd

Azar, B. (2011, April 1). Positive psychology advances, with growing pains. Monitor on Psychology, 42(4). https://www.apa.org/monitor/2011/04/positive-psychology

Bailey J. A., 2nd (2003). The foundation of self-esteem. Journal of the National Medical Association, 95(5), 388–393.

Bremner, J.D. (2006). Traumatic stress: effects on the brain. Dialogues in clinical neuroscience, 8(4), 445-461. https://doi.org/10.31887/DCNS.2006.8.4/jbremner

Frothingham, M.B. (2021). You're Not a Fraud. Here's How to Recognize and Overcome Imposter Syndrome. Simply Psychology. Retrieved from:

https://www.simplypsychology.org/imposter-syndrome.html

Guy-Evans, O. (2021). Amygdala Function and Location. Simply Psychology. Retrieved from:

https://www.simplypsychology.org/amygdala.html

Guy-Evans, O. (2021). Amygdala Hijack and the Fight or Flight Response. Simply Psychology. Retrieved from: https://www.simplypsychology.org/what-happens-during-an-amygdala-hijack.html

Merriam-Webster. (n.d.). Self-esteem. In Merriam-Webster.com dictionary. Retrieved October 16, 2022, from https://www.merriam-webster.com/dictionary/self-esteem

Merriam-Webster. (n.d.). Self-confidence. In Merriam-Webster.com dictionary. Retrieved October 17, 2022, from https://www.merriam-webster.com/dictionary/self-confidence

Merriam-Webster. (n.d.). Selfish. In Merriam-Webster.com dictionary. Retrieved September 19, 2022 from https://www.merriam-webster.com/dictionary/selfish

Merriam-Webster. (n.d.). Selfless. In Merriam-Webster.com dictionary. Retrieved September 19, 2022 from https://www.merriam-webster.com/dictionary/selfless

Merriam-Webster. (n.d.). Trauma. In Merriam-Webster.com dictionary. Retrieved October 25, 2022, from https://www.merriam-webster.com/dictionary/trauma

Merriam-Webster (n.d.). Vulnerable. In Merriam-Webster.com dictionary. Retrieved October 25, 2022 from https://www.merriam-webster.com/dictionary/vulnerable

Park, N., Peterson, C., Szvarca, D., Vander Molen, R. J., Kim, E. S., & Collon, K. (2014). Positive Psychology and Physical Health: Research and Applications. American journal of lifestyle medicine, 10(3), 200–206.

https://doi.org/10.1177/1559827614550277

Psychology Today (2022). Positive Psychology. Psychology Today. Retrieved from:

https://www.psychologytoday.com/us/basics/positive-psychology

Saraiya, T., & Lopez-Castro, T. (2016). Ashamed and Afraid: A Scoping Review of the Role of Shame in Post-Traumatic Stress Disorder (PTSD). Journal of clinical medicine, 5(11), 94. https://doi.org/10.3390/jcm5110094

Stoewen D. L. (2017). Dimensions of wellness: Change your habits, change your life. The Canadian veterinary journal = La revue veterinaire canadienne, 58(8), 861–862.

Teamphoria (n.d.). 10 Quotes on Overcoming Obstacles That Will Motivate You. Teamphoria. Retrieved from: https://www.teamphoria.com/10-quotes-on-overcoming-obstacles-that-will-motivate-you/

The University of Queensland (n.d.). Self-esteem and self-confidence. The University of Queensland Australia. Retrieved from: https://my.uq.edu.au/information-and-services/student-support/health-and-wellbeing/self-help-resources/self-esteem-and-self-confidence

University of Minnesota (2016). Daring to be Vulnerable with Brené Brown. University of Minnesota. Retrieved from:

https://www.takingcharge.csh.umn.edu/daring-be-vulnerable-brene-brown

Chapter 7

DEALING WITH STRESS AND OVERCOMING THE FEAR OF FAILURE

"Failure is another stepping stone to greatness."- Oprah Winfrey

"Failure is a part of the process. You just learn to pick yourself back up."- Michelle Obama

"When we give ourselves permission to fail, we, at the same time, give ourselves permission to excel."- Eloise Ristad.

Fear of failure is something that is very common. Anytime we try something new, have to present in front of others, or receive an answer to something that may be negative, fear can easily creep in. While fear is a normal emotion, part of our sympathetic nervous system, it can be crippling for some. In this chapter, we are going to review what fear is, how chronic stress can have an impact on our health, how to look at failure in a whole new way, and ways to alleviate chronic stress.

Fear is defined as an unpleasant, often strong emotion caused by anticipation or awareness of danger (Merriam-Webster, n.d.). Fear is an emotion that can come on in not just situations of being in danger but with situations where we have a fear of the unknown. For example, applying for a position that you really want to get. While waiting to hear back if you got the position, you may feel a high level of anxiety, not knowing what lies ahead. You're not in any physical danger, but you can be feeling these feelings for a number of reasons. You need a higher-paying job, or you want to get out of a job now that you feel is toxic. Situations like these can cause us to feel afraid and lead to uncertainty. The important thing is when we feel such emotions, to acknowledge them and know how to respond to them in a healthy way.

In order to understand fear and stress, we have to understand how the human body works and how we process emotions. Emotions come from our autonomic nervous system, one of the subsystems of the nervous system. Our nervous system is broken into subsystems, each responsible for certain functions. According to the American Psychological

Association, the nervous system is a system of neurons, nerves, tracts, and associated tissues that, together with the endocrine system, coordinates the activities of the organism in response to signals received from the internal and external environments. The two main subsystems of the nervous system are the central nervous system and the peripheral nervous system. Our central nervous system includes our brain (retina and optic nerve in our eyes) and our spinal cord (Cleveland Clinic, 2022). The peripheral nervous system consists of all the other parts of the nervous system and consists of two subsystems: the somatic nervous system and the autonomic nervous system.

The first subsystem is the somatic nervous system. Our somatic nervous system consists of our voluntary muscles, the nerves, and our senses. The one sense that is excluded from the somatic nervous system is vision because the retina and optic nerves are a part of the brain (Cleveland Clinic, 2022). The second subsystem is the autonomic nervous system which connects our brain to our internal organs.

The autonomic nervous system consists of three divisions, but we are just going to focus on two of them. The two divisions, the parasympathetic nervous system and sympathetic nervous system, play an important role in our survival. According to Cleveland Clinic, the parasympathetic nervous system is responsible for "rest-and-digest," helping you calm yourself after experiencing stress or helping to digest food when you are relaxed. Cleveland Clinic defines the sympathetic nervous system as a network of nerves that help to activate the "flight or fight" response when you are experiencing any level of stress or are in danger. Each one has a different impact on your body, with the goal of bringing balance to the body and ensuring its survival. Listed below on the chart are the effects the parasympathetic and sympathetic nervous system have on our bodies.

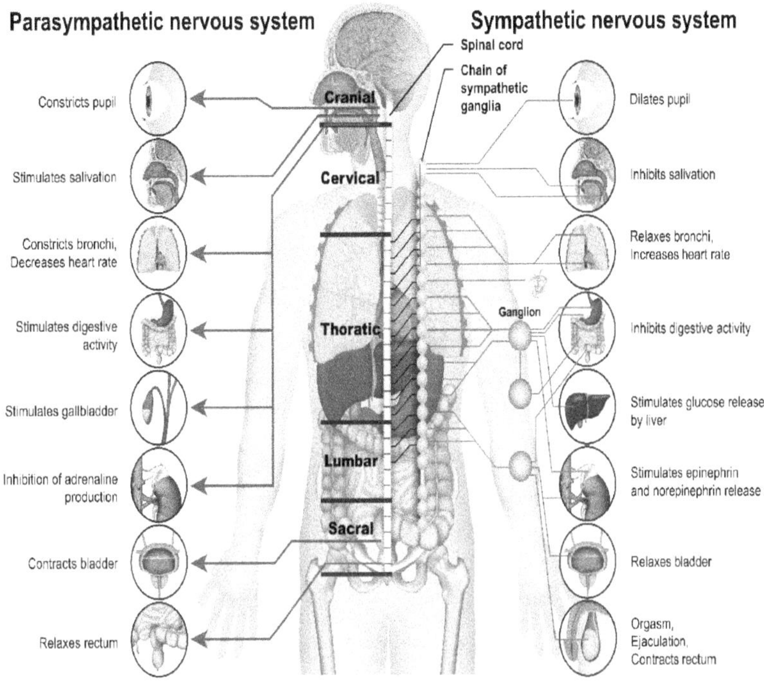

Photo Credit: www.depositphotos.com

When we do not know how to deal with stress or situations that make us fearful, it can have a very negative impact on our health. Chronic stress can lead to hormonal imbalance, which can have a harmful impact on our health and, long-term, if not addressed, can cause chronic illness and impair one's quality of life.

Cortisol, our primary stress hormone, plays an important part in how we deal with stress. According to Mayo Clinic, cortisol increases sugars (glucose) in the bloodstream, enhances the brain's use of glucose, increases the availability of substances that repair tissues, and curbs functions that would be nonessential or harmful in a fight-or-flight situation. In the article, *Chronic Stress, Cortisol Dysfunction, and Pain: A Psychoneuroendocrine Rationale for Stress Management in Pain Rehabilitation*, the authors define cortisol as a vital catabolic hormone that is produced by the adrenal cortex of the kidney. It is also a potent anti-inflammatory hormone, working to prevent inflammation which can lead to tissue and nerve damage.

Normally when we are anxious about something, we have what is known as an acute stress response. Adrenergic catecholamines, norepinephrine, and epinephrine are released, resulting in increased heart rate, blood pressure, and respiration, the arterioles constrict, sweat secretion, and pupil dilation (Hannibal and Bishop, 2014). Within fifteen minutes of stress being triggered, our amygdala activates the hypothalamic-pituitary-adrenal axis, which releases adrenocorticotropic hormone from the anterior pituitary, which then releases cortisol from the adrenal cortex (Hannibal and Bishop, 2014). Cortisol levels stay elevated, allowing the mobilization of glucose and tissue substrates for fuel, suppressing non-vital organs, and decreasing inflammation to properly manage stress levels (Hannibal and Bishop, 2014).

Now when someone is in a constant state of anxiety or fear and feels helpless, that's when stress does damage to our bodies. Chronic stress long-term can lead to many conditions, such as fibromyalgia, osteoporosis, rheumatoid arthritis, myopathy, chronic fatigue syndrome, chronic pelvic pain, and many more (Hannibal and Bishop, 2014). The difference between acute stress and chronic stress is while cortisol is released for a certain amount of time for acute stress, with chronic stress, the release is prolonged, resulting in cortisol dysfunction. Long-term effects of cortisol dysfunction include bone and muscle breakdown, fatigue, depression, pain, memory impairments, sodium-potassium dysregulation, orthostatic hypotension, and impaired pupillary light reflex (Hannibal and Bishop, 2014). Long-term cortisol dysfunction can lead to developing many forms of autoimmune diseases.

Seeing the long-term effect that stress can have on someone is an eye-opener. Stress is known as a silent killer, so why do we fail to take care of ourselves? Why do we allow fear and stress to take over? It comes down to the fact that if we want to remove fear from our lives, we must face it. That is so much more easily said than actually done. I'm the first to admit there are situations in which I could work through a situation that made me uncomfortable and some that took me years to face. At the end of the day, to remove fear and negative stress from our lives, we must take steps to face and overcome them.

One resource that can be used to help reduce stress is positive thinking. The Mayo Clinic describes positive thinking as approaching unpleasant situations in our lives in a more positive and productive way. Instead of thinking in a negative way if something doesn't go right, you take a positive approach to why it happened and how you can make things better. It comes down to self-talk or our thinking when situations occur. Instead of thinking the worst right away, it is how we can approach it and turn it into a less stressful situation.

Benefits of positive thinking include:

- Increased life span

- Lower rates of depression

- Lower levels of distress and pain

- Greater resistance to illnesses

- Better psychological and physical well-being

- Better cardiovascular health and reduced risk of death from cardiovascular disease and stroke

- Reduced risk of death from cancer

- Reduced risk of death from respiratory conditions

- Reduced risk of death from infections

- Better coping skills during hardships and times of stress

- (Mayo Clinic, 2022)

So how can you change something from negative to positive? It should be a step-by-step process, not an impulsive jump. One of the first areas Mayo Clinic suggests is finding the areas you need to make improvements. Is it your job, family members, or improving you? We can't fix everything overnight, so start simple. When I started using positive thinking as a tool, the first area I used it in was my relationship with my mother. My mother and I have never really bonded. For years, I tried to do everything I could to gain my mother's acceptance. I have lost count of how many times I broke down, became angry, and got myself all worked up just because I wanted to have a civil relationship with her. I talk to my mother a handful of times a year. I can call my mother, and she won't answer the phone. It can be months before I hear a word out of her. What led me to start practicing positive thinking regarding my mother was an argument we had. I was really frustrated with my care and situation due to the complications I was facing between epilepsy and long-haul Covid. Before going into the epilepsy monitoring unit, I let my friends know on social media what was going on. Many of my closest friends are still in New York. I explained after forty years of living with epilepsy, I was really frustrated and was hoping to get some answers. I told them if things didn't work out, I didn't want to make changes to my care and would just accept that in time, what is right now keeping me alive was going to be the end of me. My closest friends could sense I was depressed and scared of going into the hospital. My stepfather put a laughing face on the comment, knowing that I would never become seizure-free without medication. I was angry, hurt, and done with his inappropriate behavior. I took a screenshot of his name with the laughing face. I made a post showing his reaction to me being ill and stated how this was the person my mother put before her three children. I called both of them out for their behavior and made it clear I was no longer afraid of him and I had moved on. My stepfather accused me of slandering my mother, and he wanted me to take the post down. I give him credit; he did not deny what he did to my siblings and me. I told my stepfather to take a hike and that his family and my mother may enable his bad behavior, but I was not going to. He let me know that he was blocking me and never wanted to speak to me ever again. Most people would be upset that someone who was a parental figure in their life said that, but my stepfather doesn't realize he gave me the greatest gift through that response. It was the first step in breaking away from him.

A couple of days later, my sister asked me to call my mother, saying that she was upset with me. I waited until I knew I would be able to remain calm and called my mother. Her first response was she wanted me to remove the post and tell everyone that I lied to them. My response to her was clear to the point; I simply said, "The hell I will." I let her know that I was done with my stepfather's behavior and that if she wanted to continue to allow him to control her, especially after what he had done to all of us, it was her choice. She continued to make every excuse that what he did was really not that bad. I finally told her if she couldn't be a parent to me, that was fine; I would accept it. I told her, though, to step up to the plate and be there for my brother. My brother has been battling mental problems for years and has battled drug addiction, due to not trusting psychiatrists and choosing to self-medicate rather than get clean and seek a proper diagnosis. He had a relapse, and I found out from my sister that he had been abusing cocaine. He was going through horrible withdrawal. My family wanted to send him to NYU for a sleep study, and I told my mother it had nothing to do with sleep apnea. He needed to go into a dual-diagnostic center, get clean, and get a proper diagnosis. I was ready to help her with that. Instead, I was told it was none of my business, and she hung up on me. Even though it hurt to hear the phone cut off, it was the first step in putting positive thinking to work.

I will say in my brother's defence that it isn't my business when it comes to the decisions he makes when it comes to his health. I more than understand and empathize with him about his phobia of doctors, just like I have. I wish he would handle it in a different way. I love him more than anything, and the thought of him putting illegal drugs into his body is very hard to deal with. We haven't talked in a very long time, and I hope as I write this that he is clean, happy, and doing good for himself. For years I slept with my phone on my nightstand, fearing I was going to get the call that my brother had overdosed and didn't survive. It drove my husband nuts because he would tell me he could hear the phone at night if it updated something. He would ask me over and over to please turn my phone off or put it in the office. I couldn't bring myself to do either; I had to be ready just in case. This is a perfect example of allowing fear of the unknown to control me. I had to tell myself that as his sister, I could love him, and I could tell him my opinion on things, but at the end of the day, it is his life. He has to take responsibility, make his decisions, and accept the outcome. I know when he is using, his mind is not clear, but I know that I cannot get through to him, no matter how much I want to. I finally took my husband's advice and turned the phone off at night. So far, it has alleviated a lot of anxiety, and my sleep has improved. I just wish in taking this step that I knew how to do the same for my brother.

After the argument with my mother, I had to sit down and tell myself the same thing I did for my brother. I love my parents; I want them to be happy and healthy, but I cannot allow their toxicity to control my every move. I finally cut them loose and told myself that if it is meant to be, we would talk again. The result was surreal. I noticed that when I was breathing, I was not having chest tension. For years I had chronic chest tension, not heart pain, but muscular pain. It felt like someone was pushing on my chest, like someone was restricting my breathing. I blamed it on anxiety, not wanting to acknowledge that I was still allowing my parents to mentally control me and letting the past still dwell over me. It was amazing to take a breath in and not feel discomfort as I did it. It was then I realized I had broken free from their toxicity; I was free to move forward and live my life. I made up my mind I was doing just that, for my children, for my husband, and for myself.

I kept my distance from my mother throughout most of 2022. She would send gifts for my sons, and she sent me flowers for my birthday. What she fails to see is that it is just stuff; my kids would much rather talk to their grandmother than receive toys. I would text her thank you, and she would respond. It just proved what I felt, that there was no connection. When it upset me, I reminded myself that I was sleeping better and that my chest pain was gone. Did I want to take a step back or continue moving forward? It was hard not running right back to my mother like I had in the past, but I knew I needed to stand my ground.

In October of 2022, I sent my mother a message through Instagram, letting her know that I felt it was best we continued to keep our distance and the positive impact it was having on my health. I told her the physical benefits I was experiencing, such as no longer having chest pain. The one thing I did ask of her was to start talking to my sons again. As upset as I was with her, I didn't want them not to know their grandmother. I knew how much it hurt when my mother's parents were not allowed to be a part of my life, and I was not going to lower myself to that level. She reached out, and we set a date for her to call the boys. She followed through with her promise to call, and the boys were happy to hear from her. After the boys talked to my mother, we talked for around ten minutes. What I realized as we talked was how much the mood had changed. I could feel that my mother realized she had lost control and that if we were going to have a relationship, things were going to change. Since that conversation, we have talked one other time. My long-term goal is to have a civil relationship with my mother. Being angry and saying I never want to see her again would just make me bitter and set me back. When the temptation to do that sets in, I practice positive self-talk and remind myself of the benefits of making changes and continue moving forward. It's easier said than done, it took many years to do it, but I feel it's better late than never to start new habits.

There are many people who need help to take that first step in facing fear. According to Cleveland Clinic, one in ten American adults and one in five teenagers deal with a specific phobic disorder in their lifetime. Atychiphobia, known as an extreme fear of failure, is a phobia that can have a severe impact on someone's life. Atychiphobia comes from the Greek word "atyches" meaning "unfortunate" (Cleveland Clinic, 2022). There is no statistic on how many people are affected by atychiphobia (Cleveland Clinic, 2022).

For many people who develop phobias, their fears tie back to their upbringing. People who experienced during their childhood being told over and over they were not capable of doing something are at higher risk for developing a phobia. When addressing an issue like this, making improvements personally and professionally, it is very challenging and time-consuming. The best example I can give is peeling the layers off of an onion. You address an issue and work through it. You peel that layer off, and under it is another issue. It is why it can take years to have the strength to heal and move forward.

Many phobias have similarities, making them very challenging for physicians to treat. For example, atelophobia, an overwhelming fear of imperfection, can easily get mixed up with atychiphobia. The difference between the two is individuals with atelophobia will set unrealistic goals and then be upset when they don't reach them. People with atychiphobia are afraid to even try, assuming that the worst will happen.

Symptoms of Atelophobia and Atychiphobia

Symptom	Ateloph obia	Atychiph obia	Bo th
Afraid of performing simple tasks at work, home or school		X	

Angry/Irrit able			X
Anxious about being judged by others		X	
Depression			X
Pessimistic (negative outlook on life)			X
Prone to procrastination if a task or activity seems challenging		X	
Unable to maintain relationships		X	
Unwilling to accept constructive criticism or help		X	
Burnout/Fat igue	X		
Emotional Detachment	X		

Inability to accept criticism	X		
Inability to concentrate on anything apart from their fear	X		

Resource: Cleveland Clinic

The reason for showing this is that so many people are quick to label their imperfections, saying, "I can't reach my goal because…" and then giving a whole list of reasons. Phobias are learned behaviors; they come from toxic environments, abusive relationships, and traumatic experiences. Clinical approaches to unlearn a phobia, such as decoded neurofeedback, are being studied, but they are very limited and have a long way to go before being available for treatment. CyberTherapy is currently being researched with which the goal of using virtual reality to measure the biofeedback of the person and create a phobic stimulus, allowing the person to face their phobia autonomously (Lucifora et al., 2021). At this point, though, it is through treatment of cognitive behavioral therapy that people learn how to deal with phobias. Exposure therapy, also known as desensitization, is a form of cognitive behavioral therapy used to help treat phobias and reduce fears (NHS, 2022).

The first step in getting past feeling like a failure or failing at something is to change your mindset about failure. There are going to be situations in which, when you set a goal, it won't work out. That does not mean you are a failure, it means you have to go back to the drawing board, see what mistakes you made, and reset your goals. People who complain that they are failures do not take that step, missing out on the opportunity to achieve their goals. It can take time for someone to be able to set a realistic goal for themself. Here is the thing, and it is very important; I want you to give yourself permission to fail as you work to become a stronger person, both personally and professionally.

Think back to chapter three, when we discussed personal and professional goals. I gave you some examples of tools you could use to focus on your goals. One of them was a vision board. I went back to the board I made to see how much I had followed through on. Mentally I am getting stronger now that my health is improving, and I have cut back on my hours to spend more time with my kids. Working with my therapist has helped to decrease my depression, and I have less insomnia. Two of my goals are to speak in public on a regular basis and to start a second book. I am starting to work on it; I have had a few public speaking events as well as presenting online and being on a podcast. Next year, I will start the outline for my next book. One thing I didn't follow through on is having a date night once a month with Tobias. We are very overdue for that. Now, not reaching that goal doesn't make me a failure; it means I have to look at my schedule and see what changes I need to make. I also need to talk to Tobias about the importance of having time together, especially with the type of schedules we have. It is a goal that both of us should work on together. The nice thing about the vision board is that once you reach a goal, you can modify it and challenge yourself to take it to the next level. You can also simply replace it with another goal.

One of the worst things you can do to yourself or your colleagues is micromanaging. Micromanaging is managing, especially with excessive control or attention to detail (Merriam-Webster, n.d.). People who micromanage themselves or their teams cannot grow and move to the next level for one simple reason: they cannot get out of their own way. To make things worse, when employees see their leaders acting in such a way toward them, they pick up the bad habit of doing it to others. In the article, *Why Is Micromanagement So Infectious?* the authors explain that micromanaging is not just a personality or leadership trait, but it is a breakdown of delegation between a manager and employee. Let's say that a manager gives an employee a task to complete. They may give them a due date to complete it, a budget to stay in, or policies to follow (Canner and Bernstein, 2016). The point of giving the task is to be able to trust that employee to follow through with things, complete what work needs to be done, and help the company grow. Now, the manager may see that the employee is doing it in a way that they would not and takes over, telling them how to do it. The manager is now micromanaging the employee.

It is very easy to become a micromanager. I have found myself micromanaging at times, even if it was not intentional. The nonprofit that I created has a YouTube channel. I brought on a couple of interns to help me create presentations. One of the interns did a great job, and their presentation looked professional and was proficient. The other one did the basic minimum and really did not put effort into making sure it was great for our supporters. I gave the intern a second chance, and the result was just as bad, despite giving some suggestions. Knowing I wanted to monetize the channel and make it into another source of revenue for the foundation, I took over making the videos. I created the PowerPoint presentations and did the voice recording. I did the animation, scheduled the videos, put the tags in, and pretty much I took on the responsibility of the YouTube channel. At the time, I was concerned about wanting things to be proficient and professional. We have people globally looking at our channel. We also have neurologists, neurosurgeons, EEG techs, neuroscientists, and students reviewing the channel as well. Trust me; the doctors are watching to make sure that I am using creditable information, properly citing any information, and making sure I am not misguiding anyone. I knew if I screwed up and did not do it right, no one would be watching my videos due to negative feedback. At that time, the organization had not been operational for even a year. I was determined to create a creditable organization that people could trust. We have created a great channel and created four more this year. Our main channel has been monetized like we wanted. What did I get out of it, though, as a leader? By taking over the project, I micromanaged my interns and demonstrated that I did not trust them to complete the task. Even though I told them not to worry and gave them something else to do, I was wrong to act the way I did. I should have sent the work back and said in a professional manner that it didn't meet the requirements that the organization expected. I should have helped them set a goal so that they could work towards it. If they did not make the corrections I suggested, I should have met with them via zoom and asked if they were confused about anything and what I could do to help them with their assignment.? Instead, I took over, made more work for myself, and in time started experiencing burnout by taking on both my responsibilities and others. Many leaders do this. The challenge is how to set goals for yourself, not micromanage yourself and your team.

In the article, *Why Is Micromanagement So Infectious?* the authors list four elements that they suggest that the reader use to prevent micromanagement. They are:

1. **Clear Targets**

    It is important to make sure that you communicate what you want the end result to be to your teammate. In organizational leadership, creating a positive climate is something many focus on. Are you communicating with your teammate? Do they understand the task that they have been assigned? Do they understand how to get to the end result? Do they know if they can come to you with questions? Many times leaders will assign something and just expect their teammates to get it done without communicating what is expected from them. When they don't see the results they want, they go after the teammate, criticizing what was not done to their standard. The end result long-term can drive a good employee to seek employment elsewhere. Others will not want to take on any project and be under your leadership.

2.   **Sufficient (but not stifling) Constraints**

With any project or task, you want to put some level of constraint so that your teammate understands the layout of their task and what is expected. You don't want to overstep and take over the project like I did with my interns. Once you overstep and tell them what to do, when to do it, how and why, you have taken over and the task or project out of their hands. They no longer have any control to do what is expected because you are watching like a hawk to make sure they do exactly what you want. You don't want to assign something and then not communicate with your teammate, and you don't want to be standing over them, breathing down their neck. You need to find a healthy balance to establish trust, allow your teammate to learn, and, when having challenges, know that they can come to you and ask questions. Being a mentor to them or a sponsor can help to establish a healthy professional relationship and an opportunity to grow together.

3.   **A Shared Understanding**

It is important that there is a meeting of the minds when assigning a task or project to a teammate. Writing down and creating a strategic plan to get the job done is beneficial for both the leader and their teammate. Remember, you might get to the end result one way and they in another. If you want something specific, say so. At the same time, be open to hearing ideas from them. My one board member has been teaching me about the algorithm when it comes to our YouTube channels. I know that if we hadn't worked together and I hadn't listened to his suggestions, we wouldn't be at our goal now. I have been able to learn from him, and he has from me. It has been an amazing project to work on, and to see us reaching our first goals is rewarding. You want to have an awarding outcome with your teammate. Do that together by both of you contributing to the project.

4.   **Effective Oversight**

Just because you have given someone a task and a goal to complete, someone may not have the capacity to reach that goal. Again, going back to the situation with the intern that I had helping me with the PowerPoint presentations: Even though I assigned the task, the intern did not have the capacity to reach the goal. It was the first time they had been assigned a task like this. They didn't show much motivation to learn. By just stepping in and taking the project from them, short-term, it made me feel better to do it. Long-term, it now has become an extra thing to do that if I had been patient, I could have, in time, trained a couple of interns to create proficient and professional presentations.

The examples that the authors gave can also be applied to oneself. If you don't understand what you want the end result to be, you don't establish short and long-term goals and create the constraints to get to that goal. If you are not sure that you have the means to accomplish the goal, you are going to tear yourself apart and, in many cases, give up. Micromanagement is a way to create chronic stress for yourself and for others. One of the former clinical deans where Tobias works was always tearing apart many of the faculty and staff. There was high turnover because, with the consistent tension in the clinic, many felt they were being underpaid to put up with the constant negativity. One time, he went after Tobias over the suture material that was ordered. Suture material connects the soft tissues around your teeth together to help with the healing process (Yokoyama, 2021). They allow periodontists to close the wound in the surgical site and hold gum grafts in place (Yokoyama, 2021). The sutures the clinical dean wanted Tobias to order were twenty dollars cheaper than what Tobias was using. Tobias explained to him that the brand the clinical dean wanted to use had bad reviews and was known to have a higher risk of loosening or breaking apart. One thing Tobias has to be very careful about is putting his patients at risk for any level of infection. If the work does not heal right, it may need to be done again or can cause other complications. Perio surgery is not cheap, and many who travel to dental schools are in desperate need of care and cannot afford to go to a private dentist. They can wait months for their treatment. Tobias refused to use the brand the clinical dean wanted and made it clear he was not putting his patients at a high risk of complications over twenty dollars. The clinical dean was taken aback and did not want to hear Tobias' professional advice, even though the clinical dean was a general dentist and had never done surgery before. He felt as the leader of the clinic, he knew what was best and did not want to hear from his specialists what they felt was best for the patient. Needless to say, after that experience, Tobias lost a lot of respect for the clinical dean; neither one really wanted to work together, and when the clinical dean retired, Tobias was very happy because a lot of the negativity that had been taking place stopped.

Fear is something that can have a negative impact on our health, prevent us from reaching goals and growing, and can lead to us becoming insufficient leaders. Focus on practicing positive thinking and accept that you will not always win; you will not always get it right the first time. It is alright if you need to modify a goal because it was not realistic when you first wrote it. Fear is a learned behavior, and to overcome fear, we must face our fears and set goals to overcome them. Do not allow your fears to come into the workforce and cause you to micromanage yourself and others. It can drive employees with potential away and cause you to experience burnout. Refer back to chapter three and review establishing personal and professional goals to get you past any fears. Look back at the previous chapter and see if any life experiences caused you to develop any of the fears you may have. Set goals and work towards healing and gaining strength. Fears are difficult to get over, but it is possible if you put your mind to it.

Things to remember:

1.   Fear is a learned behavior. Fear can cause one to develop chronic stress, which can lead to long-term health complications. Focus on overcoming fear and practice positive thinking to help in approaching fear in a positive way.

2.   If you do not achieve a goal, it is okay. It does not make you a failure. Do not allow fear to overtake you and prevent you from having opportunities in your life and career.

3.	Do not allow fear to impact the work environment you are in. Do not micromanage yourself or your teammates. Be open to comments and suggestions, create balance, and focus on establishing a healthy climate with your teammates.

Resources:

Alfred, L. (2022). 55 Inspirational Quotes About Learning From Failure. *Hubspot.* Retrieved from: https://blog.hubspot.com/sales/learning-from-failure-quotes

American Psychological Association (2022). Nervous System. *APA Dictionary of Psychology.* Retrieved from: https://dictionary.apa.org/nervous-system

Canner, N. and Bernstein, E. (2016). Why Is Micromanagement So Infectious? *Harvard Business Review.* Retrieved from: https://hbr.org/2016/08/why-is-micromanagement-so-infectious

Cleveland Clinic (2021). Atelophobia (Fear of Imperfection). *Cleveland Clinic.* Retrieved from: https://my.clevelandclinic.org/health/diseases/21932-atelophobia-fear-of-imperfection

Cleveland Clinic (2022). Atychiphobia (Fear of Failure). *Cleveland Clinic.* Retrieved from: https://my.clevelandclinic.org/health/diseases/22555-atychiphobia-fear-of-failure

Cleveland Clinic (2022). Autonomic Nervous System. *Cleveland Clinic.* Retrieved from: https://my.clevelandclinic.org/health/body/23273-autonomic-nervous-system

Cleveland Clinic (2022). Parasympathetic Nervous System (PSNS). *Cleveland Clinic.* Retrieved from: https://my.clevelandclinic.org/health/body/23266-parasympathetic-nervous-system-psns

Cleveland Clinic (2022). Sympathetic Nervous System (SNS). *Cleveland Clinic.* Retrieved from: https://my.clevelandclinic.org/health/body/23262-sympathetic-nervous-system-sns-fight-or-flight

Cortese, A., Tanaka, S.C., Amano, K. et al. The DecNef collection, fMRI data from closed-loop decoded neurofeedback experiments. Sci Data 8, 65 (2021). https://doi.org/10.1038/s41597-021-00845-7

Deposit Photos (2022). Autonomic Nervous System picture. *Deposit Photos.* Retrieved from: https://depositphotos.com/271512130/stock-illustration-sympathetic-parasympathetic-nervous-system-medical.html

Hannibal, K. E., & Bishop, M. D. (2014). Chronic stress, cortisol dysfunction, and pain: a psychoneuroendocrine rationale for stress management in pain rehabilitation. Physical therapy, 94(12), 1816–1825. https://doi.org/10.2522/ptj.20130597

Lucifora, C. et al. (2021). Cyber-Therapy: The Use of Artificial Intelligence in Psychological Practice. In: Russo, D., Ahram, T., Karwowski, W., Di Bucchianico, G., Taiar, R. (eds) Intelligent Human Systems Integration 2021. IHSI 2021. Advances in Intelligent Systems and Computing, vol 1322. Springer, Cham. https://doi.org/10.1007/978-3-030-68017-6_19

Mayo Clinic (2022). Positive thinking: Stop negative self-talk to reduce stress. *Mayo Clinic.* Retrieved from:

https://www.mayoclinic.org/healthy-lifestyle/stress-management/in-depth/positive-thinking/art-20043950

Mayo Clinic (2021). Stress Management. *Mayo Clinic.* Retrieved from:

https://www.mayoclinic.org/healthy-lifestyle/stress-management/in-depth/stress/art-20046037

Merriam-Webster (n.d.). Fear. In *Merriam-Webster.com dictionary.* Retrieved November 13, 2022, from

https://www.merriam-webster.com/dictionary/fear

Merriam-Webster (n.d.). Micromanage. In *Merriam-Webster.com dictionary.* Retrieved November 24, 2022, from https://www.merriam-webster.com/dictionary/micromanage

National Health Service (2022). Treatment-Phobias. *National Health Services, United Kingdom.* Retrieved from: https://www.nhs.uk/mental-health/conditions/phobias/treatment/

Yokoyama, M. (2021). Dental Sutures: What Gum Surgery Patients Need To Know. *Encinitas Periodontics & Dental Implants.* Retrieved from:

https://encinitasperiodontist.com/p/BLOG-81818-2021.3.8-Dental-Sutures:-What-Gum-Surgery-Patients-Need-to-Know

Chapter 8

Sharing Your Story: We All Have One

"Sharing our truths can provide the opportunity for great healing"- Kristen Noel

"The courage it takes to share your story might be the very thing someone else needs to open their heart to hope"- unknown

"Owning our story and loving ourselves through that process is the bravest thing that we will ever do"- Brené Brown

Whether we want to believe it or not, we all have a story to share, something to contribute to society. For many, the thought of sharing their story with others can be very scary. At one point in my life, if you had asked me to share my story of battling epilepsy, I would have said no. The thought of others knowing what I was dealing with, the risk of losing my job, losing my medical benefits, and losing everything was scary. The thought of others having the opportunity to judge me for having a neurological disorder was too much. What I didn't see at that point was people could only judge me if I allowed them to. It took years before I had the strength and opportunity to move forward and start sharing my story.

There are many benefits to sharing your story. It can be overcoming something like I have, sharing a passion you have about something, someone you love who dealt with something like an illness, and now you are helping to advocate for that community; why you chose the career you have, there are many things that as humans we are passionate about. The important thing is when sharing your story, you need to be authentic, sincere, honest, and show through verbal and non-verbal communication how much this means to you. If you try to pretend that you care about something or say one thing and do another, people will notice it. Once it is noticed, your creditability is going to go down and fast. It takes a lot of time and effort to establish creditability. Once you have it, you don't want to lose it. You can lose your creditability so quickly, especially in this day and age. Think about social media and all of the crazy things that are said in posts. Things like that do not go away; they will be out and in the open forever.

Being authentic is easier said than done. We live in a society that judges you on every little thing, from how we look and what we believe to just about any little thing you can think of. Because of that, we do the craziest things to fit in and be part of the clique or group. That is one of the first steps in losing authenticity. We are so worried about being accepted by others that we have one side of us that we want everyone to like and accept and our true selves that people do not know. It is hard to be yourself because when we don't do what others feel we should, it leads to them not wanting to be around us and causes loneliness. If someone truly accepts and respects you, it will not matter what you may believe, how you may identify, or who you love. They will accept you for you, and that is what you want. Short-term, you may feel lonely and question whether you are doing the right thing. Long-term, you will see the results as people see you are honest, straightforward, and sincere. That is what leads to becoming authentic.

When I was researching for some information on authenticity, were so many different suggestions for how to be authentic it wasn't even funny. I found articles that had twenty suggestions on how to be authentic. I'm going to simplify it down to the five steps I feel would be the best approach to being authentic. This is a combination of what I have experienced personally and professionally.

Honesty is the Best Policy

As hard as it can sometimes be, being honest is the way to go. Dishonesty, passive aggressiveness, and gossiping are three things that will make you come off as not being authentic and destroy your creditability. In some situations, it may be best not to say anything or answer a question by asking one. Sometimes getting people to answer their own question can get them to open up about what they are feeling. People will remember if you are being honest with them or not. As for gossip, someone might tell you something, and by the time that gossip goes around, the story is totally different. Don't get caught in that negative circle; stay true to yourself, and others will notice.

Accept Your Imperfections, Face Your Fears

As humans, we all have strengths and weaknesses. Acknowledging our weaknesses does not make us weak; it is the first step to becoming stronger. Facing our fears, and accepting what challenges us, puts us in a situation where two things can come from it. We either suppress our fears and challenges or set goals to overcome them. Acceptance for some people can take years. Make it a mission in life to work towards being a stronger person. You are not working towards perfection; none of us are perfect. You are working towards the best person you can be for you.

Be Accepting of Others

In this lifetime, you will meet people from all different backgrounds, different cultures, different ethnicities, different faiths, and different lifestyle choices. One thing that I have seen that harms growth both personally and professionally for people is when they refuse to accept and respect other people for who they are. Extremism, no matter what level it is on, is not acceptable. You may have a co-worker or family member whose beliefs or lifestyle you do not approve of. Guess what? It's their life and their choice. That may sound harsh, but when you practice intolerance, it shows negativity, toxicity, and an unwillingness to learn and adapt to change. That's not being authentic; that's being judgmental, narrow-minded, and showing you have no room for growth. Not being able or willing to grow will backfire. You cannot force people to change their lives to what you feel is best for them. Tolerance and respect are important if you are going to practice authenticity.

Practice What You Preach, Set Healthy Boundaries

Being sincere to yourself and others is essential. One of the biggest mistakes we make is looking out for others while neglecting ourselves. No one is going to take you seriously if you are advising someone to do something and then you do the total opposite. Set healthy boundaries both personally and professionally. Do not be afraid to say no; there are times when saying no is in your best interest. You're not going to make everyone you know happy; not everyone will accept you.

There are two ways to look at that; either you are going to be bothered by it or realize you don't need their toxicity in your life. At the end of the day, taking care of yourself is an important part of being authentic. You matter, and when others see the confidence and respect you have for yourself, they will see the positivity within you, which will strengthen your credibility.

Let Your Passion Show, Allow Yourself to Shine

When we are truly passionate about what we do, it is almost impossible to hide what means so much to us. Whenever I talk about what I want to do for the epilepsy community and what I would like to see change for people with disabilities and differences, people tell me that they can truly see how passionate I am about my work. It comes naturally to me because I want to see positive change; I'm not here for fifteen minutes of fame. I didn't create my organization to get rich; I created it to create change. When something really matters to you, you don't do it for fame or fortune; you do it because you care. When people see you care, that right there makes such a positive impact.

Saying that you should be authentic is one thing; now, how do we practice being authentic? What steps do we need to take? This is where sharing your story comes into play. Sharing your story takes strength, pushes you out of your comfort zone, and shows how resilient you are. Resilience is the ability to recover from or adjust easily to misfortune or change (Merriam-Webster, n.d.). In my lifetime, I have found that the most resilient people have been through so much and over time, they turned their trauma into strength. Sharing your story, no matter what it is, will help you to become resilient, gain personal strength, and work towards healing. In the article, *Resilience and 4 Benefits to Sharing Your Story*, the author points out four benefits to building and sustaining resilience. They are:

Realizing that sharing your story can help others

Sharing your story can be therapeutic, not just for yourself but for others. When I started sharing my story, I had a number of adults who were battling epilepsy reach out to me. Many were frustrated with the lack of services, discrimination in the workforce and in healthcare, and lack of family support. Sharing your story can give others the strength they need to make a change for themselves. Talking to others who understand and can empathize with the challenges you have faced can help remove negative feelings such as feeling isolated. Use your story in a positive way to help others see past their pain and see that there is hope.

Finding Your Voice

What does it take to find your voice and share your story? Most of the time, it comes from an experience that makes you want to share your story. Mine came from an event I attended for epilepsy. Being around people who understood what I was going through and who were facing the same negative stigma I was facing gave me the strength to want to do more. Other times we find our voice due to what others experience. Recently I met a woman who lost a loved one to stomach cancer. She told me that for a long time, her loved one was sick and misdiagnosed. Once a diagnosis was made, her loved one was in stage four. She is determined to educate others and is sharing her story of what it was like to lose her loved one to cancer. She wants to make changes for better access to care and better doctor-patient relationships. Finding your voice and sharing your story can make such a difference for yourself and others.

Re-affirming Your Values

It is one thing to tell a story; it is another thing to learn from it. Understanding how your story plays into your life is important in order to share it. In sharing my story of battling epilepsy, I have learned that in order to be successful, I cannot allow epilepsy to control my every move. I had to get away from others who took a very different approach. I left many of the support groups I belonged to on Facebook. I got tired of people saying how epilepsy had destroyed them and displayed a level of bitterness due to their challenges. Epilepsy has prevented me from accomplishing some of the goals I had in life, but it has never destroyed my life simply because I refuse to allow it. Epilepsy has made me take a step back, appreciate what I have, and work towards being as independent as I can be. As a mother, I have to set a positive example for my sons and show them that we all have challenges. At the end of the day, how we approach them is how they will have an effect on us. How you approach your challenges and share them with others will determine where your values are.

Finding Peace, Finding Hope

To find peace, we have to focus on our overall well-being. Allowing ourselves to grow, to heal, to become stronger takes many steps. Even as we heal, we may take a step back before we can move forward. Use your story as a tool to heal and gain strength. There will be times when you share your story; you may feel it backfires. An example would be a time when I shared my story with an entrepreneur. He said to me, "You come off as so smart, but I would never hire you." Now I could have easily allowed this to offend me and fall apart. Instead, I told him I appreciated his honesty and asked him if he would tell me why. His argument was that if he hired me and I had a seizure on the job, I would sue him for my injuries. If one of his clients saw me have a seizure, it would traumatize them, and no one would want to do business with him. My response to him was I could understand his argument thirty years ago, but I could not support it now. I gave him an example of why his argument was not valid. If he hired me for an administration position, I wouldn't need to be on-site. I could work from home, send my work in through Dropbox, and meet weekly with him on Zoom. He wouldn't have to worry about me even being there, and he could let his customers know that he was diversifying his company and giving those with disabilities and differences a chance to be a productive member of society. He didn't know how to respond. Seeing that I put something in his mind that was not there before gave me some peace and reminded me why I am advocating for my community. I know it will take time, but I do hope in my lifetime, I can at least lay the foundation that will start to create change. I would like to see the younger generation dealing with epilepsy be able to look at what I went through and feel peace, knowing they won't have to deal with it. Yet, they can have the strength to advocate for themselves and make things even better. I'll be the first to admit that there have been times when situations like this have happened, and I've thought, "Why am I doing this to myself?" The answer is I'm working to create change. Finding peace and hope will not always come from positive experiences. The important thing is how you handle those experiences.

We can share our stories through our life actions as well. When people think of sharing their story, they think of someone doing public speaking and talking to others about it. While that is one way to do it, it is not the only way. You can share your story through your work and through the things that help you find balance.

When it comes to personal passions, they are a great way to find balance in life. We all need something that brings us happiness. Building LEGOs, exercising, gardening, hiking, and painting are the things that bring me happiness and for which I have a personal passion. I connect to each one in a different way. I have collected LEGOs since I was a child, and building sets gives me some personal space and some me time. My oldest son is passionate about LEGOs as well, and at times, we build together. Exercising helps me to keep my PTSD under control, reduces my night terrors, and decreases my panic attacks. Gardening brings me a sense of happiness when I may be having a bad day or depressed. Hiking makes me appreciate the beauty we have around us. Working from home, living in a city, it is so easy not to see how beautiful our world is. Painting has created a sense of calmness and improved my mental well-being. I enjoy creating pour paints and gifting my work to those I care about and who mean a lot to me.

It is important for all of us to find a personal passion and pursue it. The reason for that is what we do to strengthen ourselves personally or find happiness can have an impact on us as professionals. In the article, *5 Incredible, Research-Based*

Benefits of Having a Passion Outside Work, the author points out five benefits to finding a personal passion.

It Will Boost Your Performance at Work

According to the article, *The Unexpected Benefits of Pursuing a Passion Outside of Work*, there are not many professions where a career and passion can come together. In fact, making your passion and career the same things can be harmful in the long-term. It can lead to exhaustion by not being able to separate work from personal life. By separating our personal passions from work, we are able to reduce stress, increase energy, and increase levels of creativity which may boost work engagement and retention (Jachimowicz et al., 2019). In order to give your best at work, you have to do what you can to care for yourself so you can give your best.

It Will Increase Your Confidence

Researchers discovered that the more passionate people are about a hobby, the more confident they feel in other areas of their life (Stillman, 2019). As our confidence increases, it gives us the motivation to do more, and to be better. We have the strength to set goals and take things to the next level. What is beneficial about this is we are not being pressured into doing it; we are making the decision to take things to the next level.

It Will Make You More Resilient

To become more resilient, you need to be able to separate yourself from the stressors in your life. Just like people have to separate themselves from past traumas, there are some professions in which people need to be able to break away at the end of the day. Nursing is a profession that is in demand, yet its turnover rate continues to climb. According to the article *Nursing Shortage*, employment opportunities are projected to grow at a faster rate (9 percent) than all other occupations from 2016-2026 (Haddad et al., 2022). You would think, with the opportunities growing, that more people would be attracted to the profession or want to be there long-term. The truth is many hospitals understaff nurses, the result leading to burnout and high turnover. In fact, in 2021, the turnover rate for staff RNs increased 8.4 percent, resulting in a national average of 27.1 percent (Gamble, 2022).

I have two friends who are nurses and love what they do. I have had one friend work in many different areas of nursing and in many positions since starting her career. She has never been terminated and has always been a team leader, no matter where she was working. Her reason for leaving a position and going to another? Trying to find a healthy work-life balance. When she started in her career, she was working the night shift for better pay and to gain experience. In time she realized how much her job had become part of her life and did not want to miss out on her three children. Also, working in certain positions, she was being verbally abused by patients, which I could see from when she talked about it that it was having an impact on her mental health. She had no problem standing up for herself, but you could see it was a battle she didn't want to be a part of. In time she was able to find a position that allowed her to continue what she loves doing and have time for her husband and children. No matter what your profession is, at the end of the day, leave work at work and allow yourself time to recover.

It Might Make You Smarter

According to the article, research shows that these seven hobbies will make you smarter; hobbies such as playing an instrument, reading, exercising, learning a new language, cumulative learning, brain challenges such as puzzles and video games, and meditation benefit our brain in different ways. Playing an instrument strengthens the corpus callosum, creating new connections (Baldassare, 2015). Putting together puzzles increases neuroplasticity, changing neural pathways and improving cognitive abilities (Baldassare, 2015). My youngest son Anthony has taken a liking to LEGO, but differently than my older son Edward who loves to build sets with me. This year when LEGO had their second LEGO CON, a celebration from the LEGO House in Demark, we watched to see what new sets would be coming out this year. They released the Lion Knights' Castle, which, if you loved the castle sets from the 1980s, will bring back many happy memories. The two designers of the set explained all the cool things about the set and that it had taken nine years to finalize it. Tony turned to me and asked me why it would take nine years to finish one set. Going over the fine details of the set, such as the trap door at the entrance that leads to the dungeon, I had to explain the challenges of making it work. How were they able to make sure the minifigure fell down and into the dungeon correctly without getting stuck? Certain parts of the castle had very small measurements and were very detailed. I found a program through LEGO in which you can use computer-animated design to create your own characters and sets. Once Tony saw how much went into designing a set, and that it was not just throwing a bunch of bricks together, it made him want to learn more about designing sets.

It Can Serve as a Form of Mindfulness

Mindfulness is the basic human ability to be fully present, aware of where we are, what we are doing, and not to overreact or be overwhelmed by what is going on around us (mindful, 2020). Fulfilling passions that make us happy helps to alleviate stress and increase well-being. Many practice mindfulness through meditation or add it to certain activities such as yoga. Doing something that makes us happy can help us to find balance and be aware of our surroundings in a positive manner. Balance is important in maintaining overall wellness.

When it comes to passion in a professional setting, you can create passion for yourself and your teammates. This is an opportunity for one in a leadership role or wanting to get to a leadership position to be able to take their team and career to another level. Remember to keep your personal and professional passions separate and allow yourself time to recover and relax.

Think back to the beginning of your career. When you entered your field, how did you feel about your profession? Was there something you truly loved about your work? Many people enter the workforce full of passion when they complete their educational requirements. It is what happens after they enter, whether that passion stays alive or burns out. When Tobias first entered academics after finishing his Ph.D., he was so happy. He was hired to help open a new dental school. He was working long hours, wanting everything to be perfect for his students. He wanted them to have the best opportunities while going through the program. He also wanted to grow the dental school into something that would put them at a competitive advantage.

As time went on, however, those feelings turned into frustrations. Any suggestions he made to leadership were shot down. He tried to collaborate with other organizations to help get funding, but he was told to stop; that was not his job. He was being stretched between teaching periodontic classes, surgery, patient consultation, research, life science classes; you name it, Tobias was doing it. Over the years, the mistakes that were being made when the school first opened were still being made. There was no growth. The funding that kept the school going was from the student's tuition, not much more. In time his attitude went from it being his passion to now it was just a paycheck. Thankfully, it gave him the confidence to go back and pursue his MBA. Tobia's goal is to open a clinic of his own and reignite his passion by being his own boss.

It is very easy for some people to lose their passion when they are in a stressful environment. For Tobias, it has been the lack of communication and disorganization that has made him want to take the next step in his career. For others, it may be a bad boss; they are not getting paid what they are worth or realize that the position they are in has caused them to plateau, preventing them from moving up to the next level. All of these things can lead to someone losing their passion.

Even if you have lost the passion for what you are doing right now, there are ways to find your passion again. Finding your passion and what you wanted to do with your life was the beginning of your story. That passion could have happened at any time, whether it was in your childhood, during which you experienced an important life event, or as you started higher education. How has the story changed as you have gone through your career? For some, it can be an inspiring story, while for others, it may feel like a soap opera. If it is the second one, take a step back and look at the situation. What caused your passion from bringing you happiness to now you are just going with the flow? Write some notes down, create a timeline, and find where you first found that things were becoming negative. Are those situations still taking place, or have you just not let them go? If things are still the same, now may be the time to start writing down goals for what you can do to gain your passion back.

Believe it or not, you can benefit from your story just like others can. Sharing your story can help others, but at the same time, looking back at how you got where you are can help you in setting future goals. One approach to this can be using mental models. In the article, *Two Ways to Clarify Your Professional Passions*, the author gave a number of examples, with the goal of asking yourself, "What would you do and why?" A couple of examples are:

If you were a third-party giving advice to yourself, what would you suggest regarding a career choice?

If you knew you were going to be highly successful in your career, what job would you pursue today?

(Kaplan, 2015).

You may wonder why you would ask yourself such questions; why would you even approach this? The reason is this — to let go of fears, insecurities, and worrying about what others think, just focusing on yourself and pursuing the goals you desire (Kaplan, 2015). Sometimes, going over our story, seeing where we are and what we want the next chapter to be, can help us set realistic goals and see if we are happy with where we are or whether it is time to create change. Going over my own life story, I see if things had gone the way I wanted them to years ago, I would have never been able to help my community and work towards creating change. In wanting to be a trial attorney, my life would have been running in and out of court, preparing cases, and hoping to have a paralegal to help me; my life would have been my career. I wouldn't have the time to advocate, and most likely, I wouldn't due to being afraid that if people found out about my condition, my career would be over. I don't think I would have had time to even have a marriage or family. It would have been a very lonely life. When I first couldn't go on to law school, I felt like a failure; I asked myself, "Why did I even go to college?" Now, I see I am not a failure, but I hit a bump in the road and had to find the right path to go down to become successful.

There are times we share our story and don't even realize it. In 2021, I had to find a new neurologist after having some complications from Covid. After dealing with long-haul Covid and having caught a bacterial infection on top of Covid, I was really lucky I survived. The infection was giving me heart palpitations, and my brain fog was so bad I couldn't remember how to write. I was on a high level of amoxicillin for ten days while healing from the infection. While healing, I had what could have been a simple partial seizure. I had a surreal moment for about sixty seconds where I couldn't feel my body from the waist down, and it felt like my torso was detaching and leaving my body. I knew after this experience that I had to find a new doctor; I couldn't be my own neurologist anymore. Things were changing inside of me, and not for the better.

Because of the negative experiences I have had with doctors, I decided I had enough of the private practice, and I wanted to go to an academic institution to see a specialist. I tried to get into Loma Linda with a neurologist who cares for a friend of mine. My former primary care physician would not help me to appeal the denial, and frustrated; I found a new physician. A few months after, I was still having complications, and I started to look at UCLA and USC to see if there were any specialists there I felt could help me. As I was reading the bios and qualifications of all of these doctors, they all stood out. They had gone to excellent schools and had done fellowships on top of their residencies; you could tell many were in the top percentage of their class. I could tell all of them were book-smart, but the challenge was going to be communication. Would they take the time to listen? Did they have good bedside manners? One afternoon as I was looking at the specialists at USC, I came across a specialist who, when I read his bio, it put me into shock. I had never heard a doctor share his story in such a way that sounded so passionate and so sincere.

Here is my doctor's story:

"My goal is to help patients with epilepsy and other neurological disorders overcome their medical conditions and achieve their life goals. Epilepsy is a devastating disease in that it is not simply a medical illness but affects the lives of patients and their loved ones in a wide variety of ways. While advances in medical science have made many neurologic conditions treatable and, in some cases, curable, it is not sufficient to treat just the disease. One must focus on the whole person.

Furthermore, medications are just one aspect of treatment, which may include lifestyle modification, dietary therapy, and medical devices. In order to properly care for a patient, I believe a physician has to get to know their patient's values, goals, and sources of social support in the form of friends, family, and community. In this way, treatments can be targeted to each person's specific needs and desires."

(Keck Medicine of USC, G. Nune, MD, 2022)

I sat there in shock the first time I read it. In fact, I reread it a few times, just making sure what I was reading was really there. At this point, I had been dealing with epilepsy for forty-one years and never did I have a doctor who was concerned about my overall well-being. It was always, "I don't have time to answer your questions," or "Why are you questioning what I am doing? I'm the doctor, not you." I was so used to dealing with ultra-inflated egos that I had never truly established a healthy, civil doctor-patient relationship with anyone I worked with.

After reading this, I made up my mind I was going to get a consultation with this doctor. I requested a referral and was denied due to Keck Medical being out of my network. I made up my mind I was not taking no for an answer. My primary doctor and medical group tried to pressure me to give up and see someone in their network. Out of the two doctors available, I had already seen one, and the other had a review of one out of five stars. Former patients over and over said he had a history of verbal abuse and shouting. I made it clear to my primary doctor that there was no way in hell I was going to put up with that. I realized in order to get my way, I had to advocate for myself and not rely on my primary doctor. I called my HMO and stated that I wanted to be their most cost-effective patient. I wanted to work with a doctor I could trust who wouldn't be drugging me up on a ton of medication, causing me to be in and out of the hospital. I wanted to have a good quality of life, be able to work, and not be living off of the taxpayers. The fact that I put a dollar sign on my argument, that I was determined to save the insurance company money by them allowing me to see the doctor I wanted, got me my way. After two appeals and presenting an argument to the HMO, they pressured the medical group, and things were approved.

Two months after getting approval, I had an appointment with my doctor. When I first met my doctor, he presented himself in just the way he had in his bio. We talked for over two hours, he asked a lot of questions, he took the time to listen to me and never cut me off, and he did his job. You would think while that was taking place, I would be happy. Because of my past trauma, as I was watching him and we were talking, I kept thinking in the back of my mind that this was too good to be true. I was just waiting for something to happen, something that would throw everything off balance, his ego would show, and he would be just like every other neurologist I had run into. It didn't happen, though, and when I left, I felt a little numb. It was surreal. I was happy, yet I felt confused by everything. What did the future hold if we were to work together? Could I really get past the hold epilepsy has had on me, or was I just going to keep going with the flow as I had with other professionals? I didn't have the answers at that time, but I knew I needed to find them, especially with the complications I was having.

A couple of months later, I was admitted to the epilepsy monitoring unit for forty-eight hours to have an electroencephalogram (EEG). An EEG is a test in which electrodes are pasted onto your scalp, and the machine reads your brain waves. If someone has a seizure, the machine will pick up the overactivity, letting doctors know what is taking place so they can make decisions on what treatment options are available. My doctor's goals were simple; he wanted to get the test results, make sure my treatment was working, and create a care plan. Being there, I felt I was in an environment where they could stop my medication, see where things were coming from, and see if something like surgery was an option. Because my seizures have been controlled for so long, surgery is not an option. My emotions, however, were getting in the way of things. Common sense told me one thing; my emotions told me another. As my test was going on for two days, I did everything I could to try to get around my doctor, determined to get my way. When he wouldn't stop my meds, I tried to get him to at least reduce them to get some level of overactivity. He dug his heels in and, in a professional way, let me know he was not changing his stance on things. The morning I left the hospital, he let me know they hadn't found anything and that he was going to discharge me. At that moment, I felt I had lost total control and that I needed to find out something while there. I began to argue with him and told him I didn't want to go home; I needed to find out what was going on. When he saw I was no longer there to reason, but I was ready to start a fight, he left the room. At that point, I felt crushed; I felt like he had just walked off on me. I left the hospital, not being able to say a thing on the car ride home. Once home, I was up for over thirty hours, not being able to calm down. I had two massive panic attacks and then slept for a couple of days, getting up just enough to take my meds and keep hydrated. It took me falling apart and making myself sick to open my eyes and face reality. I realized that epilepsy was going to be a part of my life, a part of my journey until I died. Like it or not, it was not going away. Second, my doctor had not walked off on me, he saw that I was in a position where I couldn't reason, and I needed my space. Being able to look back at that moment and picturing him walking out of the room, his body language didn't say, "I don't have time to deal with this. I don't have time for patients like this." His body language said, "Girl, until you get out of your own way, how am I supposed to do my job? How can I help you reach your goals when you won't listen and take my advice?" I realized at that moment that I had overstepped my bounds, and there was a chance that he wouldn't work with me again. I knew I had to make things right.

A month after my visit, we met by telemedicine, and I took responsibility for my actions. I asked if he was comfortable working with me, and he said yes. It made me happy to know that he did not take what had happened personally and could see past what had happened. Since that time, my neurologist has been a wonderful physician and a wonderful advocate for me. I developed fibromyalgia after having complications with long-haul Covid. I was in so much pain it was impairing me from doing my work. I felt he was the only one who would understand what I was feeling, and I knew he would believe me. I've had so many doctors in the past tell me that things I was experiencing were 'all in my head.' When I told him, I was not well, instead of saying something like, "This is out of my scope; you need to talk to your primary doctor," instead he said, "We need to get you over to pain management and start getting some tests done." He helped me to get a consultation with pain management and the rheumatologist to get a proper diagnosis. When the insurance company tried to give me a hard time, he had his team on things to make sure what I needed was taken care of. Thanks to my doctor, I am now in a fraction of the pain I was in. I'm in physical therapy, and I'm getting stronger. His support gave me the strength to go back to seeing a psychologist so I could continue to focus on my overall health. Through my doctor sharing his story, it helped me to see that there are good people in the medical profession. There are physicians who are passionate and do not see their patients as subjects from whom to collect data, but as the human beings that they are. Sharing your story can touch someone in so many positive ways giving them a sense of hope and the strength to make changes for themselves for the better.

Sharing your story can help you to heal, to grow, and to make yourself into a stronger person. Be authentic and honest, and allow yourself to grow and to shine. Find passions that can help you to grow and help you find balance. Sharing your story can be therapeutic not just for yourself but for others as well. You may not think sharing your passions, desires, or goals with others can create change, but as you can see through the stories I shared here, they can create change.

Things to remember:

Being authentic is essential. Being yourself, being honest, and being sincere is needed for you to establish credibility.

Find personal and professional passions to help you maintain balance. Keep those passions separate. As important as your career may be, you need a personal passion to be able to rest and find balance at all levels.

Sharing your story can help you grow and heal, and can do the same for others. Take the step to share your story to help yourself grow and to make a positive difference for others.

Resources:

Baldassarre, C. (2015). Research shows that these 7 hobbies will make you smarter. Insider. Retrieved from: https://www.businessinsider.com/research-shows-that-these-7-hobbies-will-make-you-smarter-2015-8

Gamble, M. (2022). The cost of nurse turnover in 23 numbers. Becker's Hospital Review. Retrieved from:

https://www.beckershospitalreview.com/finance/the-cost-of-nurse-turnover-in-23-numbers.html

Haddad LM, Annamaraju P, Toney-Butler TJ. Nursing Shortage. [Updated 2022 Feb 22]. In: StatPearls [Internet]. Treasure Island (FL): StatPearls Publishing; 2022 Jan-. Available from:

https://www.ncbi.nlm.nih.gov/books/NBK493175/

Hamby, S. (2013). Resilience and 4 Benefits to Sharing Your Story. Psychology Today. Retrieved from:

https://www.psychologytoday.com/us/blog/the-web-violence/201309/resilience-and-4-benefits-sharing-your-story

Healey, J. (2018). 20 Quotes about Sharing Your Story, Baring Your Heart & Healing Hurts. Healing Brave. Retrieved from: https://healingbrave.com/blogs/all/quotes-about-sharing-your-story

Jachimowicz, J.M., He, J., and Arango, J. (2019). The Unexpected Benefits of Pursuing a Passion Outside of Work. Harvard Business Review. Retrieved from:

https://hbr.org/2019/11/the-unexpected-benefits-of-pursuing-a-passion-outside-of-work

Kaplan, R.S. (2015). Two Ways to Clarify Your Professional Passions. Harvard Business Review. Retrieved from: https://hbr.org/2015/03/two-ways-to-clarify-your-professional-passions

Keck Medicine of USC (2022). George Nune, MD, Neurology. Keck Medicine of USC. Retrieved from:

https://providers.keckmedicine.org/provider/George+Nune/20 5693#about

Merriam-Webster. (n.d.). Resilience. In Merriam-Webster.com dictionary. Retrieved December 3, 2022, from

https://www.merriam-webster.com/dictionary/resilience

Mindful (2020). What is Mindfulness? Mindful. Retrieved from: https://www.mindful.org/what-is-mindfulness/

Stillman, J. (2019). 5 Incredible, Research-Backed Benefits of Having a Passion Outside Work. Inc. Retrieved from: https://www.inc.com/jessica-stillman/5-incredible-research-backed-benefits-of-having-a-passion-outside-work.html

Chapter 9

PREPARING YOURSELF FOR SUCCESS

"I believe that people make their own luck by great preparation and good strategy." - Jack Canfield

"Success depends upon previous preparation, and without such preparation, there is sure to be failure." - Confucius

"Wisdom is nothing but a preparation of the soul, a capacity, a secret art of thinking, feeling and breathing thoughts of unity at every moment of life." - Hermann Hesse

Now that we have talked about the tools and resources needed to reach goals, what do we have to do to use them effectively? This chapter is going to focus on that. There are many situations in which it will take time to achieve a goal, or you may need to make major changes to achieve that goal. I want you to use this chapter to start laying down the foundation and building on that foundation successfully. This is going to be the start of you reaching the goals you desire.

The first step is acknowledging that you need to make a change to start working towards your goals. Until you are ready to step out of your comfort zone, things are not going to go anywhere. As simple as it may sound, for many, it is the hardest part. Looking at yourself on the inside and saying to yourself, "I know I can do better and be better," is a very hard thing to do. The first thing to look at is where you start when it comes to creating change. In the article, *22 Microhabits That Will*

Completely Change Your Life in a Year, the author listed habits she felt would be beneficial in changing one's life. I picked my favorites from the article to share with you.

Choose comfort for your future self over comfort right now

This was one of my favorites for so many reasons. I have met so many people who are more worried about keeping up with everyone when it comes to material things than they are about long-term success in life. One of my friends, when she graduated with her bachelor's degree in psychology, invited Tobias and me to be there. Her aunt met us for the first time, and when she found out that Tobias was a dentist, she said to my friend, "She doesn't come off as a doctor's wife." My friend told her she was right because I am a very independent person. The reason for this? One, I do not like to show off anything, especially material items such as cars, clothing, jewelry, nothing that draws attention. Second, by thinking long-term of how you want your life to be, it helps you to make better decisions for yourself. The reason I live simply and save what I can is I know once I no longer want to work, I want to be able to provide for myself. I don't want my children ever to have to provide for me. As much as I love working, I want to be able, at a certain age, to semi-retire, be able to travel, and do what I want when I want. To do that, I need to set goals to make it happen, which means I'm driving a Toyota Corolla instead of a Mercedes-Benz. Ask yourself, "What do you want to do in the future when it comes to finances, health, family, or anything you feel is important?" Pick something and start making the changes to make that goal possible.

Be less reactive

This has been one of the hardest things for me to learn. I'm grateful to my friend Eddy for helping me strengthen this goal for myself. Eddy and I have very similar personalities. We are honest, straightforward, hard-working, and we are passionate when it comes to our work. I have a bad habit when I work with people; I hold them to the same standard that I hold myself. Clearly, that is not possible. There are plenty of times I have gotten frustrated with people and have been straightforward with them about it. One time Eddy called me and told me never to contact someone when I was frustrated, especially through email. He told me if I could not relax, to write an email to that person, but to send it to him. When the time was right, and I felt better, to communicate when I would not come off as negative. This is important because it takes just one negative experience to ruin a personal or professional relationship. If you come off as angry or controlling, people will do what they can to avoid you. If someone does something to upset you, take a step back. Why is the situation upsetting you? Is it something personal or an unethical act? Before reacting, think about what the consequence will be. Once you feel balanced, then act on it. Do not act in any negative form. Working not to be impulsive can help us grow and become stronger.

Read more

I read every day and make an effort to learn something new. Reading daily is a wonderful habit to develop because you are gaining knowledge, reducing stress, improving focus, and it is a great form of entertainment when you just want to be alone. Read what makes you happy, whether it's fictional, history, comics, romance, or anything that helps to relax you and make you happy. My reason for reading is to keep my brain active due to my brain injury. I enjoy reading educational books, motivational books, business magazines, and more. I drive Tobias nuts when we travel because before we board the plane, I must stop at the magazine store and get the latest copy of *The Economist* and *Harvard Business Review*. If you don't have time to sit down and read, listen to an audiobook on the way to work. Keep your brain active and healthy; it will change your well-being for the better.

Observe your patterns

See what you are doing on a daily basis in life. Are there any bad habits that you need to end? What changes can you make in your daily life that will benefit you overall? Once I was diagnosed with Fibromyalgia, I had to improve my sleeping habits. I would stay up late at night at times to get ahead on work if needed. The next day, I would have a horrible flare-up, and what I could get done was very limited. I realized in time, like it or not, I had to stop working at nine in the evening. Even if I could not fall asleep right away, I had to be done. It drives me nuts because my brain is still very active, but since listening to my body, I wake up pain-free. Bad habits impact us in a negative way. Take a step back and see what you can work on to better yourself.

Practice saying "no"

This is another one that so many, including myself, have a hard time doing. Get into the habit of saying no when needed. If I said yes to every little thing people want me to do, I would never leave my seat; I would be living in my office, which is the best way to put it. If you want to help someone, set realistic goals to plan and help. Eddy has asked me to grow the YouTube channel for the chamber in 2023. I will help by submitting 1-2 videos a month for their channel. Eddy's goal is to have 100 new videos up in 2023, but I will only be contributing 12-24 at the most. I know I can't do more with my schedule, and I cannot let my responsibilities fall to the side to make others happy. If he asks for more than that, the answer will be no. Find a balance in what you can do, and if you cannot do something for someone, be honest and say no. Your health, well-being, and responsibilities to yourself come first.

Share your ideas consistently and clearly

Many people are hesitant to share ideas, worried about what others may say or think about them. If you want to move up as a leader, if you want to grow as a person, you cannot remain silent. If you have an idea that may benefit your team at work, put the idea together, how it will benefit your work, and the timeline to carry it out. Rather than just saying something, show how it can be done. Remaining silent can result in lost opportunities.

Create open portals for people to reach and contact you for what you want to do

You want to market yourself to create opportunities. LinkedIn is a great tool for just that. Make sure you are keeping up to date on your page, and as you work to grow and expand, you are adding that to your page. Anytime I complete a certification, I add it to my page. If I write an article, I add it to my page. Any volunteer work and so on gets added to my page. The point is you need to show others you are working to better yourself; you are willing to grow, you can step out of your comfort zone, and have the strength to be successful.

Begin each day by asking yourself, "How can I change my life today?"

This is a question I encourage you to ask yourself. It is one of the questions I ask myself all the time. At times, we need to take a step back and ask what we can do for ourselves to make things better. It can be focusing on improving our health, improving a relationship, letting go of toxicity, or experiencing something special with someone we care about. What I love about this question is it puts you in control of your destiny. What can you do for you? You're not being selfish in asking this question, you are looking out for yourself as a human being, and there are many situations in life where you have to put yourself first to survive. Always ask yourself what you can do for you to make a positive impact for yourself and even others.

Creating change is important for you to be able to grow and achieve your goals. What is even more important is how you create change and with who. Depending on your field, you want to network with the right people and use the available resources to your advantage. No matter what level you are at in your career, it is important to establish support systems to help you grow and move to the next level.

One of the first tools you can use to grow professionally is LinkedIn. LinkedIn was created in 2002 and officially launched in 2003. The mission of LinkedIn is to connect the world's professionals to make them more productive and successful (LinkedIn, 2022). Microsoft purchased LinkedIn in 2016 for 26.2

billion dollars or 196 dollars per share in 2016. What was started in the living room of Reid Hoffman became a multi-billion-dollar networking resource.

Think of LinkedIn as a resource to make a positive first impression on professionals you work with and future professionals you do not know yet. An image on LinkedIn is very important. It is easy not to look at your LinkedIn page for a long time yet be making changes in your career. Keep your page looking up-to-date and professional. The first thing that people are going to see is your story. You want your story not to just say what you do but why. Depending on your profession, some people keep it short and sweet, while others make it more of a story. Here are two examples for you to see.

This first one is Tobias' from his LinkedIn profile. Tobias has worked for different universities and private practices, as well as being an advisory board member for my nonprofit organization. His focus in all of these areas that he has worked in is periodontics. Because of that, he keeps his about section very simple and focuses on sharing his vision:

"My current vision is to promote health by providing excellent periodontal and implant treatments, training the next generation of dentists who are competent in diagnosing and treating periodontal diseases, and advocate for improved health care access and collaboration between health care providers, patients, and communities at large."

(LinkedIn profile, Dr. Tobias Boehm, 2022)

Tobias' vision says what he does and why. He provides care and wants to make sure patients have the treatment they deserve, make sure the next generation of professionals will be proficient in providing care and advocate to create a win-win situation for both patients and providers. It gets right to the point. Now, if Tobias owned his own practice, he would want something longer and more detailed because he would not just be sharing his vision, but he would also be marketing himself.

Now here is my story from my LinkedIn profile. It is much longer than Tobias', but I am sharing my work, mission, and life experience to establish evidence of why I felt it was necessary to start a nonprofit organization. If I did not have a business, my layout would be very different. Also, I am getting ready to launch an LLC in 2023, so as I launch my for-profit company, I will have to change my story again. As we grow, we need to adapt to the changes we are making. Here is my current story:

"I am an advocate for individuals and families who are battling epilepsy. I was diagnosed with epilepsy at the age of two due to a traumatic brain injury. For many years epilepsy had control of me, limiting me in what I could do with my life. After years of battling seizures and going through many combinations of treatments, I made up my mind that epilepsy was not going to control me. I would not allow the stigma that is associated with epilepsy to take over my life.

In 2004, after years of trying different medications, I became seizure-free. I have accomplished many things in life I was told would never be possible. I went to college and established a career. I married my best friend, and we have two sons. I am able to drive and support myself. For years despite my success, I hid having epilepsy for fear of losing my job, losing access to care. It took years before I realized in order to make a change for those with epilepsy, I had to be honest about my condition and show others despite having epilepsy, people can be successful and have a productive life.

In 2018 I decided to pursue my MBA, and in 2019 started to create *The Defeating Epilepsy Foundation*. After graduating with my MBA in 2020, we launched and began our work. Our mission is to provide the advocacy and educational resources needed by the epilepsy community and our society. Over the years, many organizations have become less focused on the community and more on pharmaceuticals, research, and working toward a cure. While that is very important and necessary, many people with epilepsy are not receiving the care they need. The result has had a negative impact on our community.

Due to the lack of education about epilepsy, many people do not understand what epilepsy is or that it even exists. Because of this, people with epilepsy face a very negative stigma causing unnecessary discrimination. Because of this, we need to help create resources for people with epilepsy and their caregivers to help increase educational and economic opportunities, improve quality of life, and in many situations, save a life.

Currently, we provide a scholarship for students battling epilepsy, as well as educational resources through our blog and YouTube channels in English, Spanish, French, Chinese, and Arabic. In 2023, we will launch our Workforce Development program to help those battling neurological and neurodivergent conditions gain the tools needed to find gainful employment. We will continue to find resources for the epilepsy community to help reach our goals and do what we can to make a positive impact."

(LinkedIn profile, Natalie Aswad Boehm, 2022)

Now, compared to Tobias' profile, my story is huge. There is a reason for my providing all of this information. There are many nonprofits throughout the United States. According to Zippia, there are over 1.5 million nonprofits in the United States, so I must establish a reason why people should support mine, whether it is through donations, sponsorship, or volunteering. Also, the challenge I have is the epilepsy community is very underserved, affecting only one percent of the population. Many people are affected by other conditions, such as cancer. Yearly, 150,000 Americans are diagnosed with epilepsy compared to 1.9 million with cancer. There is more funding for cancer research than there is for epilepsy. I think everyone has met someone who is battling cancer and sadly has lost someone special to them, a friend or family, that battled cancer. Because it is more known and affects more people, they are more likely to give to a cancer organization before epilepsy. Many people who give to my organization either have epilepsy, have a loved one with it or lost someone to sudden unexplained death due to epilepsy (SUDEP). I have had some people inspired by my work who are not affected by epilepsy donate time or resources, but many of them are local and want to see those in my local community get services. Because of this, I must demonstrate the importance of my work by sharing my personal experience, the impact it has on others, and what needs to be done to not just help those with epilepsy but help communities and our society to remove the negative impact epilepsy has on all of them. I knew sharing my story came with a high risk. After graduating with my MBA, I had a ton of companies looking at my profile; corporations, financial companies, banks, you name it. All they had to see was the word epilepsy, and they moved on. They didn't see someone who did not want to be dependent on the taxpayers of America; they didn't see someone who wanted to create change; they saw a liability. I knew by launching my nonprofit organization and sharing my story, I was going to become unemployable to many. It is why before launching my organization, I had plans to create a for-profit company as well to support myself. I knew I had two choices, become my own boss and make a difference or remain silent and establish a career with a corporation. I have no regrets about the route I have chosen and would do it all over again.

There are many benefits to building a LinkedIn page and networking. It can create job opportunities, partnerships, collaboration with organizations, and more. The only thing I don't like about LinkedIn is how many people will solicit through messenger. I know we all have to make a living, but I cannot even begin to describe to you how many messages I get weekly from people. Don't dismiss people, yet at the same time, look over their profile and see if you can truly benefit from using their services. It is best to do your homework before even responding. A lot of times, I have found that the services they are trying to sell me I can do on my own for a fraction of the cost or even free. There are people I have connected to because of their experience and connections, my mentor being one of them. He has helped me learn and grow, and that is someone you want to be in your network. You don't want people who are just selling themselves out to make money; you want to connect to others who have the same ethics and values as you do. When it comes to your LinkedIn page, make sure you are coming off as genuine, professional, and experienced. Make sure your information is organized, and make sure to make an effort to post and respond to other posts in your network. It takes time and effort, but it will help you to grow and connect to others. Social media takes a lot of work, but in this day and age, it is necessary.

Along with your LinkedIn page, a strong resume can make a difference. Building a resume can be a challenge for many. I strongly feel that they should teach all students in high school how to create a resume when they enter their freshman year. When I was in high school, there was no mention of a resume, how to prepare for college, nothing. It was that you had to attend class, and the rest was on you and your parents. I grew up in a depressed economy in upstate New York, so I feel that was a good part of it. My children are now in elementary school, so I do not know what the school districts are requiring of high school students now, but I hope it is much more than what they required my generation to do.

The reason I feel so strongly about resume writing is that this is a document that describes you. It is a tool that can create many opportunities for you when structured the right way. There is no perfect layout for a resume because there are so many different professions. The first thing I would recommend is to have your current resume reviewed to see if you are missing any important words or have any weaknesses in your resume. If you are on a budget, you can find a free resume review service. According to the article, Free Resume Review: Top 10 Online Services, these are the top ten free resume review sites:

Resume Worded https://resumeworded.com/score

Jobscan   https://www.jobscan.co/

TopResume   https://www.topresume.com/resume-review

Zipjob https://www.zipjob.com/free-review/

Hiration   https://www.hiration.com/job-search/free-resume-review/

Ladders https://www.theladders.com/resume-reviewer

Monster https://www.monster.com/resume-assessment

EnhanCV   https://enhancv.com/resources/resume-checker/

LiveCareer https://www.livecareer.com/resume/check

Employment BOOST

 https://employmentboost.com/free-resume-review-evaluation/

(Case, A., 2022)

In reviewing the article, there were pros and cons to all ten sites. Some took some time to review everything; it was not instant. In other situations, they would review so much, but for certain things, they wanted to charge for, so it was not free if you used certain tools. Review what resources are available to you and use what is best for you. Grammarly is a great resource for writing, grammar, and punctuation.

(https://www.grammarly.com/), and the best thing is that it is free.

One resource I have used is the *Knock 'em Dead* book on resumes. The book is a great collection of different resume styles and what you should consider putting into your resume. Employment, education, experience, volunteer/community service, languages, certifications, and professional skills are something I look for in resumes. One thing you should avoid putting into your resume is your religious faith, marital status, how many children you have, personal details such as health, political affiliations, or anything that can cause someone looking at your resume to judge you and deny you an interview. There are some things you want to keep private.

One thing you want to have in place before taking the step to create change is having the support system you need. Support systems come in many forms. Friends, families, support groups, and colleagues, there are many ways we can find support as we are working to grow. It is important to establish healthy relationships both personally and professionally in order to have the support you need. If you feel you are lacking support, here are some suggestions that can help.

When it comes to personal support, I have found that Tobias and my sons offer me the greatest support. Along with them, I belong to a few organizations that have support groups, and we meet through zoom on a weekly basis. I have found since Covid, that zoom is now an amazing way to connect to others when I cannot meet in person. For me, zoom has alleviated a lot of loneliness in my life. I wish it had been around twenty to twenty-five years ago when I was unable to drive. I meet with my groups two to three days a week. We talk about family, well-being, work, personal goals, relationships, and more. There are times it is just to share information and at times to ask an opinion of something. Interacting with others is very important for our overall health and for many, it can decrease depression and other negative symptoms.

According to the University at Buffalo School of Social Work, the following are some great ways to establish a support system:

Volunteer

Volunteering is rewarding on so many levels. According to Western Connecticut State University, volunteering can improve both physical and mental health by increasing self-confidence, combating depression, and helping to stay in good physical health. Before creating my nonprofit organization, I volunteered in hospitals, nonprofit organizations, and at church. Volunteering can allow you to create new friendships while making a difference in your community. Plus, it is great to be able to put down on your resume that you take the time to help others. It shows good character. The best thing now is if you cannot volunteer in person, more positions are opening up virtually, giving you more options.

Take up a sport or join a gym

Taking part in sports or exercise is beneficial on so many levels, helping to improve physical and mental well-being. It is also a great way to connect to others like you and create strong friendships. When I lived in Buffalo, it was snowing most of the year. Many people battled seasonal affective disorder, pretty much hibernating inside of their homes until spring came and the snow melted. Having depression, I knew that this was not an option for me. I started doing Tae Kwon Do as a way to exercise, not sit around my apartment depressed, and be around others. It was challenging and allowed me to set goals for myself for physical and mental strength. Even though I haven't lived in Buffalo now for twelve years, many of the people I practiced martial arts with I am still in contact with and have remained great friends. Dance schools, swim schools, martial arts, tennis clubs, and gyms all have activities that adults can take part in. If you have never taken part in sports, start simple. A lot of small businesses will have trials for you to come and see if it is for you. Find something that can help you grow and connect to others.

Start a book club

Book clubs are a great way for you to read about different subjects, have open conversations with others, strengthen critical thinking, learn, and grow. There are many different book clubs you can join online if you cannot find one in person. One book club site called *Bookclubs* (https://www.bookclubs.com) helps people join and create book clubs, gain access to in-person and online clubs, and find books and events. *Bookclubs* is sponsored, allowing them to provide all services free to the community.

Meet your neighbors and co-workers

This is a great suggestion, but I feel it depends on location and profession. I feel that this way of establishing a support system has been challenging for me since leaving New York. Growing up in New York, we knew all of our neighbors. All of the kids played together. If someone had a baby, we helped the family; the same thing if someone passed, there was a system. Now when I left New York and moved to the Inland Empire, it was a whole different story. I tried to say good morning to my neighbors, and I had some who would continue to walk by, or I even had a couple roll their eyes at me as if I was bothering them. Southern California has areas that are very welcoming, but some are also very tight-knit and are not welcoming to outsiders. For a long time, I felt very lonely here. I met people who moved from Los Angeles because it was cheaper within a year to move back to the city due to the lack of socialization in the area. It comes down to location. When it comes to co-workers, if you can establish friendships with them, I encourage you to do so. It helps create positivity in the work climate, and they can become a strong support system.

Join Professional Organizations

Professional organizations are a great way to establish connections but also create friendships with those you have things in common with. Before joining any organization, especially if they are ones where you pay an annual membership fee, do your homework. Depending on their size and what benefits they can offer can determine what is best for you. For individuals who own their own company, a Chamber of Commerce is an excellent resource. Depending on your target market and location, you should decide if your local city chamber is best for your business or do you want to be involved in a larger regional one that will have more connections. To be a member of a regional chamber will cost you more, but you will get what you pay for. If you don't own a business but want to be involved in the professional community, organizations such as the Rotary Club are beneficial. One of the local Rotary Clubs I am affiliated with fundraises to provide books and school supplies for the schools in their district. Becoming involved with an organization such as a Rotary Club can help to create professional friendships, network, and provide meaning. It also looks good on your resume, just as volunteering does.

Use online resources

Social networking sites, such as Facebook and Instagram, have been used to keep in touch with friends and family as well as make new friends. Like anything, there are pros and cons to social networking sites. Facebook Messenger has been great for me over the years to keep in touch with my friends out East. If we cannot talk on the phone, we can send a message. I have also made friends on Facebook as well. I can say though in all of the years, I have made friends on Facebook, I have only met two. One of them has epilepsy, like me, and we met at an Epilepsy Convention three years ago. The other person I was friends with for two years before we met. There are many nice people on social media, and there are also some scammers. Social networking sites can be a great resource, but use caution when meeting new people, even if it is just through the network.

Another way to meet others is through Philanthropy. When people hear the word Philanthropy, they automatically think of someone like Bill Gates or Warren Buffet, someone who gives millions of dollars to a cause. You don't have to be a billionaire to become a philanthropist. Philanthropy is defined as goodwill to fellow members of the human race, an act or gift done or made for humanitarian purposes (Merriam-Webster, n.d.).

There is a difference between Philanthropy and charity. An example of charity would be donating winter coats or funds one time to a local shelter. Philanthropy is volunteering on a regular basis for an organization or giving funds for a particular cause on an annual basis. According to the article, *What is Philanthropy? Examples, History, Benefits, and Types* in the United States, religious organizations, education, and human services receive the most amount of funding. People give to a cause that is important to them, allowing them to help make a difference. Giving is not only good for those we help but for ourselves as well. According to Cleveland Clinic, when we do good for others, neurotransmitters such as serotonin, dopamine, and oxytocin are released, which regulate our mood, give us a sense of pleasure, and create a sense of connection with others. Other benefits are a decrease in blood pressure, a longer lifespan, and a boost in self-esteem and happiness (Cleveland Clinic, 2022).

Make sure if you become involved in Philanthropy; you are doing it for the right reasons and not just to add something great to your resume. There are many local organizations that people start because they have been affected by a certain illness or life-changing event. These small organizations are just as important as the larger national ones, if not more. Many of the larger nonprofits are receiving funding from the government and universities or are involved with lobbying. Many smaller local nonprofits are helping people directly in the local community and are trying to bring awareness to individuals and families who are facing challenges and are relying on donations and microgrants. Take some time to look at your local community. Is there an organization that is working on something that is close to your heart? Are they involved in any projects that have a positive impact on those in need? If there is, take some time first to reach out and see how serious they are about their work. There are many small organizations that are very limited in what they do. There are some that really want to take things to the next level but just need to find the right supporters. Even if you start by volunteering, you are doing good. Over the years, I have volunteered and donated to many organizations, some for a number of years. I have volunteered for hospice, I'm an advocate for LGBTQ+ rights, an advocate for animal rights, I sponsored a child in Sierra Leone for five years, I am a guardian for the Erie County Animal Shelter, and I contribute to my organization. I can say that what Cleveland Clinic says about giving is true. Even though I have faced my share of hardship in my life, nothing makes me happier than helping those who deserve to have a better life and better opportunities. I have met a lot of wonderful people over the years when helping others. When you are around others who enjoy helping others as well, it is so fulfilling. Set a goal to find a local organization whose purpose is meaningful and start helping them to make a difference.

If you are a business owner, it is even more important for you to be involved in Philanthropy. According to the San Diego Foundation, corporate Philanthropy refers to investments and activities that a company voluntarily takes on as a responsibility to help make an impact on society. Target has its employees volunteer to help local organizations at events. Walmart has microgrants of up to five thousand dollars for smaller organizations to put towards programs. Just because your company does not have the same value as Target or

Walmart does not mean you cannot do good for your community. For example, if you are a catering company and a local charity wants to have an event, you can offer to cater for the event. Prepare an invoice for them with the costs of helping them and request a receipt. Make sure their tax number is on the receipt so you have things in order. When you give an end-of-the-year report to your customers or clients, you can share that this is one of the many wonderful things you did for the community over the year.

According to the San Diego Foundation, the seven most common types of Corporate Philanthropy are:

—	Matching Gifts: Companies financially match donations that their employees make to nonprofit organizations.

—	Volunteer Grants: Companies provide monetary grants to organizations where employees regularly volunteer.

—	Employee and Board Grant Stipends: Corporations award grants to employees and/or public boards to donate to the nonprofit of their choice.

—	Community Grants: Company programs award nonprofit organizations that apply for grants based on defined criteria.

—	Volunteer Support Initiatives: Companies partner their employees with nonprofits that provide specialized support.

—	Corporate Sponsorships: Companies provide financial support to a nonprofit that, in return, acknowledges that the business has supported their activities, programs, or events.

—   Corporate Scholarships: Corporations provide scholarship dollars to universities on behalf of students seeking support to continue their studies, encouraging college education and workforce development.

All of these options are a great way to give back to your community. Like I said, you don't have to be Bill Gates to do this. You can agree to match a fundraiser for a local charity or sponsor a project that a nonprofit has. There are many ways you can become a philanthropist and establish a positive image for your company.

For larger companies, corporate social responsibility is something that has been debated for a long time. Corporate social responsibility is defined as a self-regulating business model that helps a company be socially accountable to itself, its stakeholders, and the public (Fernando, 2022). There have been many debates about corporate social responsibility. Researchers like Milton Friedman felt that companies had a responsibility for their profits to go to their shareholders, to focus on the growth of a company, not what society was dealing with. There are many ways for larger companies to practice corporate social responsibility, which benefits both the company and society. One of the ways that many companies are practicing social responsibility now is through implementing diversity, equity, and inclusion (DEI) in their companies. Because of the complexity that DEI can bring, it is mostly multinational companies that are investing in DEI directors and stronger human resources to make their goals possible. Companies such as MasterCard have taken the step to make DEI an important part of their mission.

"We are on a journey to create a workplace and world where everyone has equal access to connect their greatest passions with their fullest potential. That starts with our people and how we lead, with a sense of decency and inclusion." – Michael Miebach, CEO of Mastercard

The reason for putting this in is to show you that no matter what level you are at, there is always a situation in which you can make a difference. If you are an employee, an employer of a small company or a multinational company, there is always a reason to connect with others and to help make a positive impact. Do not allow where you are now to stop you from growing and making it to the next level. Where you are now is your foundation. Now is the time to start building on it.

Things to remember:

To be able to create change, you have to acknowledge you need to make change. Be ready to step out of your comfort zone because that is how change is going to happen.

Use the proper tools to grow and develop yourself into a stronger person and professional. As you grow, do not forget to do things to care for yourself.

Charity, Philanthropy, and corporate social responsibility all play important roles in creating change for the better. No matter what level you are at in your career, make it a goal to give to those in need. It benefits both them and you.

Resources:

American Cancer Society (2022). Cancer Facts & Figures 2022. American Cancer Society. Retrieved from: https://www.cancer.org/research/cancer-facts-statistics/all-cancer-facts-figures/cancer-facts-figures-2022.html

Ariella, S. (2022). 25 Incredible Nonprofit Statistics [2022]: How Many Nonprofits Are In The US? Zippia. Retrieved from: https://www.zippia.com/advice/nonprofit-statistics/

Bloomenthal, A. (2021). Resume Definition: Meaning, Purpose, and What Should Not Be On Yours. Investopedia. Retrieved from:

https://www.investopedia.com/terms/r/resume.asp

Bookclubs (2022). About Us. Bookclubs. Retrieved from:

https://bookclubs.com/about

Case, A. (2022). Free Resume Review: Top 10 Online Services. ResumeGenius. Retrieved from:

https://resumegenius.com/blog/resume-help/free-resume-review#jobscan

Cleveland Clinic (2022). Why Giving Is Good for Your Health. Cleveland Clinic. Retrieved from: https://health.clevelandclinic.org/why-giving-is-good-for-your-health/

Fernando, J. (2022). Corporate Social Responsibility (CSR) Explained with Examples. Investopedia. Retrieved from: https://www.investopedia.com/terms/c/corp-social-responsibility.asp

Hayes, A. (2022). What is Philanthropy? Examples, History, Benefits, and Types. Investopedia. Retrieved from: https://www.investopedia.com/terms/p/philanthropy.asp

LinkedIn (2022). About LinkedIn. LinkedIn. Retrieved from:

https://aboutlinkedin.com

LinkedIn (2022). Profile for Dr. Tobias Boehm. LinkedIn. Retrieved from: https://www.linkedin.com/in/drtobiasboehm/

LinkedIn (2022). Profile for Natalie Aswad Boehm. LinkedIn. Retrieved from: https://www.linkedin.com/in/natalie-aswad-boehm-mba-rblp-t-ab4782161/

Mastercard (2022). Diversity, Equity, Inclusion, Creating limitless possibilities for everyone. Mastercard. Retrieved from: https://www.mastercard.us/en-us/vision/who-we-are/diversity-inclusion.html

Merriam-Webster. (n.d.). Philanthropy. In Merriam-Webster.com dictionary. Retrieved January 2, 2023, from

https://www.merriam-webster.com/dictionary/philanthropy

San Diego Foundation (2022). What is Corporate Philanthropy? San Diego Foundation. Retrieved from: https://www.sdfoundation.org/news-events/sdf-news/what-is-corporate-philanthropy/

Sullivan, D. and Holland, K. (2019). Epilepsy: Facts, Statistics, and You. Healthline. Retrieved from: https://www.healthline.com/health/epilepsy/facts-statistics-infographic

Tweedie, S. (2016). Microsoft Buys LinkedIn for $26.2 Billion. Business Insider. Retrieved from: https://www.businessinsider.com/microsoft-buys-linkedin-2016-6

University at Buffalo (2023). Developing Your Support System. University at Buffalo, School of Social Work. Retrieved from:

https://socialwork.buffalo.edu/resources/self-care-starter-kit/additional-self-care-resources/developing-your-support-system.html

Western Connecticut State University (2022). Community Engagement, Benefits of Community Service. Western Connecticut State University. Retrieved from:

https://www.wcsu.edu/community-engagement/benefits-of-volunteering/

Wiest, B. (2018). 22 Microhabits That Will Completely Change Your Life in a Year. Forbes. Retrieved from: https://www.forbes.com/sites/briannawiest/2018/09/18/22-microhabits-that-will-completely-change-your-life-in-2-years/?sh=c61f48d10354

Williams, S. (2022). 90 Preparation Quotes to Help You Reach Your Goals. Everyday Power. Retrieved from: https://everydaypower.com/preparation-quotes/

Yate, M. (2016). Knock 'em Dead Resumes (12th ed.). Adams Media.

Chapter 10

WHERE TO GO FROM HERE

"Don't dwell on what went wrong. Instead, focus on what to do next. Spend your energy moving forward together towards an answer"- Denis Waitley

"The only thing a person can ever really do is keep moving forward. Take that big leap forward without hesitation, without once looking back. Simply forget the past and forge toward the future"

- Alyson Noel

"If you can't fly then run, if you can't run then walk, if you can't walk then crawl, but whatever you do you have to keep moving forward"- Martin Luther King, Jr.

Using the tools in this book and the experiences you have personally and professionally, you are now taking the first steps to build yourself up to build your brand. Whether you work for a company or are your own boss, everyone needs to build their brand. Building a brand for yourself is easier said than done. In fact, it has been one of the most challenging things for me.

When I first launched my organization, I was very assertive in networking and getting to know the professionals that are working in the epilepsy community or were retired and still engaged. Before launching my organization, I had been active in social media, talking to people with epilepsy. I felt a lot of frustration that people were not getting the answers they needed. I was asking people what they felt was lacking when it came to educational resources and services for people with epilepsy. My goal was to find out where there was miscommunication between people with epilepsy and the medical community and how to strategically plan to help open the communication lines long-term. I knew the probability was low at this point, mainly because it would require people to change, something most people refuse to do.

Three months after I launched the organization, I caught Covid. Where I am living in Inland Empire, despite the governor putting a mask mandate into place, the county sheriff let citizens know that he would not cite them if they didn't follow the mask requirements. It put everyone at risk, but especially elderly people and people with disabilities and differences, both groups have many people who are immunocompromised. I sought medical attention at the emergency room and was not taken seriously. I ended up catching a bacterial infection on top of Covid and was not aware that I had it. I thought it was just Covid complications, and despite being sick, I kept working daily, determined to gather the information I needed and start putting resources together for the community. Slowly my health started to deteriorate to the point where just typing at my computer took everything out of me. I was working on a project helping one of my professors. I took a position for a year as a research assistant, helping my professor gather data. I sat down to write my paper and submit the data and just looked at the computer. I stared at the APA template and did not know what to do. I had no understanding of how to write a paper, despite research and writing being my passion. I knew then something was seriously wrong, and if I didn't get things together, I was not going to survive. I was able to get in touch with the Covid state team and was put on a high level of antibiotics for ten days. At that point, my focus was getting rid of the infection to get my health together. It became one of the most challenging times in my life. There were days I couldn't get much work done. I didn't want to make videos or take pictures of myself for social media. I felt very weak and didn't want anyone to see me in that state. Instead of sharing my journey in fighting Covid complications and showing the importance of taking preventative steps not to spread it, I hid in my home, wanting more than anything to get past things.

Now, most people would think what I did was right. No one needed to see me at such a vulnerable time. I had interns helping build the social media with infographics, we launched our YouTube channel, we were building our blog, and we were accepting applications for our first scholarship award. Most people would say a lot was going on, and we were laying the foundation to build upon. I didn't do the right thing, though; in fact, I didn't for a very long time. While healing, I found my comfort zone of being behind my computer writing papers, doing research, mentoring interns, and keeping out of the limelight. Many people, including my interns, told me I needed to start making videos and talking to the community. Many felt being the founder of the organization, I needed to get on social media such as Instagram live. The excuse that I gave everyone was that it was not about me, that the organization was a gift from me to the community, and it was about the community. The truth was that I was embarrassed about the state I was in. I took myself off the road and refused to drive for seven months. I was in pain and physically weak; I had to lie down after lunch daily if I was going to make my afternoon appointments. My health on all levels had deteriorated. I didn't want to admit I was depressed, but I was. I was nowhere near where I really needed to be.

Looking back at the situation, I really wish I had not taken the route I did. At times I was going on podcasts and having group discussions with professionals, but that is only one piece of the puzzle. I wasn't making videos for the community, I was not having live discussions, and I was only doing a fraction of what was expected of me. When I was writing the sixth chapter of this book, I realized how many of the topics and situations I wrote about reminded me of the amount of healing I still had to do. As part of it, I had to start making more of an effort to get past things.

The reason this is so important is because if you don't work to brand yourself, others in time will. You want to be focused on what you want to be known for, your skills, and how working with others will benefit them. In the article, *10 Golden Rules of Personal Branding*, the author lists ten important steps you need to take to personally brand yourself.

Have a focus

It is important for you to find your calling, what you are known for. Trying to be all over the place will result in burnout and not reaching your target audience. My focus is strategic planning and advocacy. I help people strategically plan personal and professional goals to help them gain strength and make positive changes in their life — advocate to help others overcome their struggles and find their voice. My passion is helping people, especially those who fall under DEI, find their voice, gain confidence and strength, and take things to the next level. Keep things simple when it comes to your focus so that people know who you are and what you do. It creates opportunities that otherwise can very easily be missed.

Be genuine

You will hear over and over again how important it is to be authentic, be genuine to others. That's because this is so important when establishing a brand. If you try to be someone you are not, it will be remembered and very damaging. Recently in the news, George Santos, the representative in the 3rd congressional district of New York, lied on his resume about his education, his career, his income, and more. One of the many things that Santos lied about that really upset me was that he claimed that he was Jewish and his grandparents fled Ukraine and then Belgium to escape the Holocaust, when in fact, none of that happened. The New York Post published an article in which Santos stated, *"I never claimed to be Jewish. I am Catholic. Because I learned my maternal family had a Jewish background, I said I was Jew-ish."* (Nava and Campanile, 2022). I'm not even Jewish, and I can say it infuriates me to think someone would use a sensitive topic such as the Holocaust for political gain. Most people have enough common sense not to do something as egregious as Santos, but the best advice I can give you is this; don't be a Santos, be a genuine person.

Tell a story

Telling your story is the first step in getting your brand built and established. Why are you doing what you do? When I showed you my story on my LinkedIn profile in Chapter 8, that is just one example of sharing your story. When I talk in public or initiate conversations with professionals, I briefly share my story in introducing myself. The reason for this is that I want them to know what my organization stands for, why I created it, and what my long-term goals are. I keep things consistent and straight to the point. That way, people know what I stand for. Be ready to share your story.

Be consistent

One thing I love that the author points out is how important it is to demonstrate consistency and how tiny inconsistencies can derail establishing your personal brand. Also, you need to work both online and offline in establishing your brand. Online, I post articles on LinkedIn daily; I post information on our social media channels, doing what I can to keep our audience engaged and find potential supporters. Another way of establishing consistency is a tool such as a mascot or catchphrase. The catchphrase I created for the foundation is *'together we will defeat epilepsy.'* The reason for this is I want to remind anyone who watches my interviews on YouTube or reads my posts to remember what my goal is in my work. I am not looking for a cure; I'm looking for a way to help others not to allow epilepsy to take over their lives. I want them to have happy, productive lives and defeat the negativities that epilepsy can cause someone. Also, I cannot do it alone; that is why I say *'together.'* Creating change cannot come from one person; it takes many to collaborate to make a difference. Keep consistent when sharing your message.

Be ready to fail

Because of how important it truly is, I dedicated an entire chapter to this one subject. If you are not ready to acknowledge mistakes and that you may not hit every goal you make, you are going to physically and mentally burn yourself out, putting your health and well-being at risk. The goal is to learn from your mistakes and try again. If you don't reach a goal, go back and try to find out why then try again. Labeling yourself a failure when you don't succeed at something will result in you giving up, and you will not be able to establish your brand.

Create a positive impact

As you grow and strengthen your brand, remember to work to make a positive impact. You can create a positive impact through collaboration, volunteering, being a board member, and more. No matter what you are doing in your career, it is important as a professional to create a positive image for yourself. Short-term, it may seem time-consuming to do these things, but it comes with long-term benefits.

Follow a successful example

Do your research and review examples of successful professionals who have established a brand. What do you see them doing? How are they sharing their story through their posts? Don't focus on just one person, such as one celebrity you like. View other professionals and what they do. It can help you to get an idea of how to start establishing your brand and what tools or approaches work best for you.

Live your brand

This is so important because you want to practice what you preach. If you want people to take you seriously, you need to demonstrate through your work and life decisions that you are an example for your audience. Establishing yourself as a leader, mentoring others, giving back to your community are examples of what you can do to live your brand.

Let other people tell your story

It is one thing to tell your story; it is another thing when people share it. When people are inspired by your story and work, they will let others know about it. One of the things I am working on now is getting over the fear of recording myself. One project I am working on is creating a playlist for the foundation channel to help people with epilepsy build skills to advocate for themselves. Videos are one of many ways to get your story across. You have only so much time in person; you have to take advantage of the resources available and market yourself. When you do, and someone is inspired by your work, they can share it; if you have a YouTube channel, they can like and subscribe, and long term, you can find ways to monetize this and create additional sources of revenue. Do well, and others will be a source of marketing for you and will help build your reputation.

Leave a legacy

What do you want to be remembered for? If there is one positive impact you can leave on others, what would it be? These are questions you have to ask yourself as you develop and grow as a leader. My goal in creating my organization is that I want the next generation dealing with epilepsy not to have to face the same hardship and discrimination that I have. I want them to look at what I have gone through and say to themselves, *"I am glad I never had to deal with those situations."* I want to lay the foundation to create change and give them the opportunity to build on that change. I know what I am aiming for will take a lifetime, and even then, I won't be able to complete everything that needs to be done. Think about what positive changes you can make and set goals to do just that.

To brand yourself, many of the tools and topics we have discussed in this book are going to come into play. Just looking at the branding suggestions shows how important all these topics are, from setting your goals, caring for yourself, overcoming your fears, and sharing your story. To be able to brand yourself long-term, you need to clearly understand the process of planning and carrying out your plan. In the third chapter, I explained the importance of strategic planning and showed you examples of how to plan using SMART. What I want you to understand as well is the background of strategic planning and not to fear it. One thing I also want you to understand is how to think strategically, learn the skills to do so, and be able to put the two together and benefit from them.

When I was working to obtain my MBA, I decided to take the strategy capstone. I felt it would be beneficial since I wanted to create a business. My classmates and I were following a program in which we were executives of a company that made chips for computers in automobiles. One person had to do research and development, another had to forecast how much we would sell and at what price, another had to put together how many workers we needed, and finally, the finances such as paying back loans or borrowing if needed. The goal was to be the team with the highest revenue in the week. There were a total of six teams competing.

This was an eight-week class, and I will admit four of the eight weeks, I felt I was on pins and needles. I just wanted to be done. This was the last class, and I wanted to finish strong and have my degree. Each week we were assigned a different thing, and I quickly learned my strengths and weaknesses. In research and budget planning, I was awesome. In scheduling people and trying to prevent overtime, I did okay, but I was scared of forecasting. I found myself doing research on these chips, trying to figure out what was a reasonable price. What really threw me off was predicting how many we could sell. For many, this is an area that creates a lot of fear. The reason is it's a fear of the unknown. Are your prices where they should be, is the quality of your product better than your average competitor's? Now, I had no idea what the other team was putting together, so I couldn't compare what they were doing as many companies could. That was the mental game I was having, not knowing what the end-of-week results would be. Some weeks we did fantastically; some, it looked like we had no idea what to do. To call it a learning experience is an understatement. This class made all of us grow; we had no choice but to step out of our comfort zones if we wanted to graduate.

My professor, who works in venture capital, watched from a distance the first couple of weeks to see whether we were really trying or just throwing a bunch of things together with the goal of just getting through the class. He saw that my team really wanted to learn. We met weekly with him, and after the first half of the class, he asked us where we had grown and what did we feel we were still lacking. I admitted to him my fear of forecasting. He could see it was not so much the forecasting, but it was the fear of failing. He explained to me that forecasting is never perfect; it is always changing because technology is changing, products change, there is always a level of change going on, and it is something that you need to be ready to adapt to.

I can say that during the last four weeks of the class, I really enjoyed knowing that what I was going through was a normal experience and that this class was laying a foundation to grow upon, improve my critical thinking skills, work towards being able to adapt to change, and not to fear it. That is how I want you to be able to approach strategic planning; it's always changing, your numbers will not always be where you want them to be, and you will be stepping out of your comfort zone, but you will grow and develop into a strong, productive leader who can critically think and is confident in taking the steps needed to succeed.

Because your plan will always be changing, you have to be able and willing to educate yourself to be able to change your mindset. That is why it is important to work to build strategic thinking skills. Strategic thinking skills are skills that enable you to use critical thinking to solve complex problems and plan for the future (Stobierski, 2020). In the article, *How to Demonstrate Your Strategic Thinking Skills*, the author points out the differences between developing strategic thinking skills and then being able to demonstrate them:

Developing Strategic Thinking Skills

In order to develop strategic thinking skills, you are going to do a number of things. It's one thing to read the information or take a certificate and say to others that you have knowledge about strategic thinking. It's a whole new ballgame when you are expected to be part of a team and put your knowledge to work. Working on a team is awesome because you can learn from your colleagues, suggest different ideas, and gain experience. One thing the author pointed out is that in leadership development programs, many of them require job rotations, cross-functional projects, and having face time with leadership (Bowman, 2019). Think back to the story I just shared with you about the capstone I took. Our professor didn't advise us to pick one thing and stick with that. We had to take part in each and every part of that project. As I pointed out in my personal experience, some things came naturally to me, and I loved working on them. Then having to forecast, there were nights I sat at my computer ready to pull my hair out. Meeting with our professor helped our team recognize our strengths and weaknesses and work towards developing better skills. Work towards developing your skills and practice what you are learning. It's one thing to be book smart; applying your knowledge is a whole different level.

Demonstrating Strategic Thinking Skills

There are many ways to demonstrate strategic thinking skills, whether it is promoting change in how a project is carried out or how your team will structure a project. Other examples that the author provided were in marketing or sales. Depending on who your client is, you have to be able to put together a plan that will meet their needs and goals. In professions such as marketing or sales, it is not a one size fits all situation. Some clients may have something simple such as promoting a business. Others may be working to take their business to the next level. Many more factors are going to come into play. This is a situation in which not only can you show your client that you have the capability to use strategic thinking skills, but your supervisors and team will see that you can adapt and make the necessary changes to help clients reach their goals.

Regarding the differences between developing and demonstrating strategic thinking skills, what can you do to develop these skills? In the article, *Strategic Thinking: The Pathway to The Top*, the author points out five things that can help you do just that:

Communicate Powerfully

To communicate powerfully, you are doing more than just listening to someone or telling them something. This is an opportunity to improve your research skills and share your knowledge with others. Bringing knowledge to the table and educating others on how to strategically put things into place benefits not only them but you as well. This is a great way to learn, grow, and help your teammates or clients to do the same.

Foster Innovation

Change is always going to happen, no matter in what field you are. Take the step of being a leader in helping your team make changes to projects or help clients learn to make changes to their business to stay ahead of their competitors. If you wait until your competitors make a change, they now have an advantage over you. Recently in the media, it was announced that Exxon Mobil has been working on predicting global warming projections as far back as 1977. Using the tests and results they conducted between 1977 to 2003, Exxon (before they merged with Mobil) predicted that temperatures would rise 0.36 degrees Fahrenheit (0.2 degrees Celsius) per decade (Briscoe, 2023). NASA has stated that since 1981, the average temperature has risen 0.32 degrees Fahrenheit (0.18 degrees Celsius), almost identical numbers (Briscoe, 2023). Seeing this information, one might ask, why didn't ExxonMobil start investing in creating other energy solutions? It was the result of many leaders claiming that the projections were not proven or that researchers were speculating, casting doubt on scientific research. Despite ExxonMobil publicly acknowledging that climate change was occurring in 2007 due to the burning of fossil fuels, former CEO Rex Tillerson questioned the climate projections (Briscoe, 2023).

The reason for these actions is that short-term, ExxonMobil leaders were focused on one thing, bringing in revenue and getting more people to invest in their stock. They didn't think long-term that if they worked to reduce carbon emissions, they could have long-term monopolized the market with products that could reduce climate change, creating a level of revenue to which their competitors would not have had access. In fact, on their corporate website, they posted that they completed the roadmaps to work towards net-zero emissions in 2022 (ExxonMobil, 2022). By not being willing to embrace change when they had the chance, ExxonMobil lost out on an economic opportunity and more. They could have used this situation to promote corporate social responsibility working towards creating quality products while caring for our environment. There is so much that could have been done to benefit both the corporation and the world. The result of thinking short-term and not being willing to create change has resulted in creating damage to our environment and damaging the reputation of ExxonMobil.

Focus on Customers

In this part, the author focused on customers, but this is something that can be applied to many professions. For the people you deal with, whether they are customers, clients, or patients, the most important thing you need to do is listen. These people understand what they are dealing with on a daily basis, whether it is the operation of a business or their health and well-being. In order to help them reach their goals, you need to listen to be able to put a plan in place and advise them. You will be respected and appreciated if you take the time to take their needs seriously.

Inspire and Motivate

It's one thing to say things that inspire people; it's a whole new level when you implement it. This is one of the things that I enjoy about working for a charity. It's one thing to say you want to make a difference. When you are able and have the evidence to show others, not only is it a great feeling, but it is a great motivator to get others involved. This can be applied when it comes to leading a team. Inspire your team to give one hundred percent, create a positive climate, and communicate and support your team, and it will motivate them to be productive and take your team to another level.

Establish Stretch Goals

This is one goal I would wait to use until you feel confident about using the SMART goal system. The reason for this is a stretch goal is focused on a high-risk goal and takes a great deal of effort. You are setting a goal that is higher than the average goal you would set; this is a goal that you may not reach the first couple of times. The best advice I can give when you go to establish a stretch goal is to break it up into a few short-term goals. You can easily get overwhelmed just by knowing it is a high risk, so make sure to take the right approach.

As you work towards branding yourself, setting goals to achieve, and understanding how to implement them, remember the importance of self-care. If things start getting to you, you start doubting yourself; I want you to go back to chapters six and seven. So many people become so focused on work, family, and other responsibilities that they forget to care for themselves. You will not be able to reach goals and move forward until you focus on your well-being and healing. Short-term, it may seem like you can, but long-term, it will catch up with you.

The reason I encourage you to go back to these two chapters is due to a lot of my experiences in my life. I neglected myself a lot in my early life, being more concerned about what others felt or what they thought. The result was self-harm by neglecting myself. The wake-up call for me was when I got seriously ill a couple of years ago and, this year got diagnosed with fibromyalgia due to experiencing severe chronic pain. You do not want to make the same mistakes that I have made and so many others do. I hope that sharing my personal stories about the struggles with my own health will give you the motivation to take care of yourself. At the end of the day, we all have challenges, but it is how we face them that matters.

For those of you who like to take notes and write down your goals, a workbook will be available to go with this book. I encourage you to get one and use it if you feel it will benefit you as you work to grow and become a stronger person. Also, go back and review the resources that I have provided. I also encourage you to do your own research when it comes to the topics in the book. There is so much information available. When we take control of our lives and invest in ourselves, we have the capacity to do so much more.

By finishing this book, you have taken the first step in helping yourself to grow and do good for yourself and others. I hope in sharing my story and the resources I have, you have been able to see that despite our challenges in life, we all have potential, and we have the capability to do something great with our lives. I refuse to allow epilepsy to stop me from achieving my dreams and any challenges you may be facing, do not let them get in the way of what you want out of life. Now be your best advocate and show the world what you are truly capable of achieving.

Things to Remember:

Branding is an important part of how you develop and grow yourself as a professional. Take control of what you want to be known for.

Make sure to understand the differences between strategic planning and strategic thinking. That way, you will understand how to use and apply them.

Remember to practice self-care and focus on your overall well-being. Use this book as a resource in helping you set and achieve goals. Go up and beyond and do additional research. Continuing to educate yourself will put you at an advantage.

Resources:

Bowman, N. (2019). How to Demonstrate Your Strategic Thinking Skills. Harvard Business Review. Retrieved from: https://hbr.org/2019/09/how-to-demonstrate-your-strategic-thinking-skills

Briscoe, T. (2023. Exxon Mobil publicly denied global warming for years but quietly predicted it. Los Angeles Times. Retrieved from:

https://www.latimes.com/environment/story/2023-01-12/exxonmobil-accurately-predicted-effects-of-global-warming

Chan, G. (2018). 10 Golden Rules of Personal Branding. Forbes. Retrieved from:

https://www.forbes.com/sites/goldiechan/2018/11/08/10-golden-rules-personal-branding/?sh=2080563658a7

Edberg, H. (2022). 40 Moving Forward Quotes (+ My 5 Favorite Tips to Move Forward). The Positivity Blog. Retrieved from: https://www.positivityblog.com/moving-forward-quotes/

ExxonMobil (2022). Advancing Climate Solutions: Net-zero ambition. ExxonMobil. Retrieved from:

https://corporate.exxonmobil.com/climate-solutions/advancing-climate-solutions

Folkman, J. (2021). Strategic Thinking: The Pathway to the Top. Forbes. Retrieved from:

https://www.forbes.com/sites/joefolkman/2021/02/05/strategic-thinking-the-pathway-to-the-top/?sh=257b9c426553

Nava, V. and Campanile C. (2022). Liar Rep.-elect George Santos admits fabricating key details of his bio. New York Post. Retrieved from: https://nypost.com/2022/12/26/rep-elect-george-santos-admits-fabricating-key-details-of-his-bio/

Stobierski, T. (2020). 4 Ways to Develop Your Strategic Thinking Skills. Harvard Business School Online. Retrieved from: https://online.hbs.edu/blog/post/how-to-develop-strategic-thinking-skills